BTEC
Entry 3/Level 1

HEALTH & SOCIAL CARE

ENTRY LEVEL 3/1

Jade Roots | Lynda Tann | Linda Winter

Teaching Book and Resource Disk

A PEARSON COMPANY

BC 00150 1178

Published by Pearson Education Limited, a company incorporated in England and Wales, having its registered office at Edinburgh Gate, Harlow, Essex, CM20 2JE. Registered company number: 872828

www.pearsonschoolsandfecolleges.co.uk

Edexcel is a registered trademark of Edexcel Limited

Text © Jade Roots, Lynda Tann and Linda Winter

First published 2010

13 12 11 10
10 9 8 7 6 5 4 3 2 1

British Library Cataloguing in Publication Data
A catalogue record for this book is available from the British Library

ISBN 978 1 846 90936 8

Edited by Philippa Boxer
Designed by Pearson Education Limited
Typeset by Tek-Art
Cover design by Pearson Education Limited
Cover photo/illustration © Westend 61 · Getty Images
Back cover photos © Westend 61 · Getty Images

Printed in the UK by Ashford Colour Press Ltd

Disclaimer
This material has been published on behalf of Edexcel and offers high-quality support for the delivery of Edexcel qualifications.

This does not mean that the material is essential to achieve any Edexcel qualification, nor does it mean that it is the only suitable material available to support any Edexcel qualification. Edexcel material will not be used verbatim in setting any Edexcel examination or assessment. Any resource lists produced by Edexcel shall include this and other appropriate resources.

Copies of official specifications for all Edexcel qualifications may be found on the Edexcel website: www.edexcel.com

Contents

About your BTEC E3/L1 Health and Social Care Student Book

About the author

Jade Roots is a Senior Tutor and Lecturer of Health and Social Care at South Downs College in Hampshire. She has broad experience teaching Level 1 BTEC qualifications in Health and Social Care.

Lynda Tann is a Lecturer and Tutor of Health and Social Care at South Downs College in Hampshire. She has managed BTEC L1 Health and Social Care qualifications and currently manages the BTEC Level 2 Diploma in Health and Social Care at her centre.

Linda Winter is Head of Social Science at Ridgeway School in Plymouth. She has taught Health and Social Care at pre-16 level and Psychology and Sociology at post-16 level.

Credits

The publisher would like to thank the following for their kind permission to reproduce their photographs:
(Key: b-bottom; c-centre; l-left; r-right; t-top)

1 Pearson Education Ltd: Mind Studio. **2 Alamy Images:** David Hoffman Photo Library. **4 Pearson Education Ltd:** Jules Selmes. **7 Pearson Education Ltd:** Mind Studio. **8 Alamy Images:** Photofusion Picture Library. **10 Pearson Education Ltd:** Jules Selmes. **12 Pearson Education Ltd:** Mind Studio. **14 Alamy Images:** Roman Milert. **19 Getty Images:** Jupiter Images. **20 Getty Images:** Bloomberg. **22 Science Photo Library Ltd. 24 Getty Images:** Dan Kitwood. **27 Getty Images:** Christopher Furlong. **28 Getty Images:** Barcroft Media. **31 Science Photo Library Ltd:** JIM VARNEY. **32 Science Photo Library Ltd:** GUSTOIMAGES. **34 Science Photo Library Ltd:** Mark Thomas. **39 Corbis:** Jim Craigmyle. **41 Alamy Images:** keith morris. **43 Alamy Images:** Catchlight Visual Services. **44 Alamy Images:** The Photolibrary Wales / Jeff Tucker. **46 Alamy Images:** Megapress. **51 Shutterstock:** absolut. **52 Getty Images:** WireImage / Danny Martindale. **54 Shutterstock:** Vatikaki. **56 Alamy Images:** imagebroker. **58 Alamy Images:** Dean Mitchell (tr). **Shutterstock:** Yuri Arcurs (b). **61 Shutterstock:** Monkey Business Images. **62 Alamy Images:** Nicole Hall. **67 Alamy Images:** moodboard. **69 Alamy Images:** Johnny Greig people. **72 Alamy Images:** Paul Doyle. **74 Alamy Images:** Blend Images. **76 Alamy Images:** Chris Howes / Wild Places Photography. **81 Corbis:** moodboard. **83 Getty Images:** Nicole Hill. **84 Alamy Images:** Christina Kennedy. **86 Alamy Images:** Peter Alvey. **88 Alamy Images:** Nick Turner. **91 Alamy Images:** Dennis Hallinan. **92 Alamy Images:** Stock Connection Blue. **94 Alamy Images:** Blend Images. **98 Alamy Images:** Butch Martin. **100 Alamy Images:** Angela Hampton Picture Library. **103 Shutterstock:** Andresr. **104 Alamy Images:** Duncan Davis. **106 Getty Images:** Jose Luis Pelaez. **108 Alamy Images:** Bill Bachmann. **111 Shutterstock:** Lisa F. Young. **112 Alamy Images:** jacky chapman. **118 Pearson Education Ltd:** Jules Selmes. **120 Alamy Images:** Form Advertising. **123 Getty Images:** Chris Leschinsky. **124 Alamy Images:** Paula Solloway. **126 Photolibrary.com:** Jiri Hubatka. **128 Getty Images:** Digital Vision / Manchan. **130 Getty Images:** Design Pics. **132 Getty Images:** Taxi / Bill Losh. **135 Getty Images:** The Image Bank / Michael Prince. **136 Pearson Education Ltd:** Lord & Leverett. **138 Getty Images:** Oli Scarff. **145 Alamy Images:** Tony May Images. **150 Corbis:** Pascal Broze / Onoky. **154 Alamy Images:** Jack Sullivan. **156 Alamy Images:** MBI. **158 Getty Images:** Photographer's Choice RF / Adam Gault. **160 Alamy Images:** JG Photography. **162 Getty Images:** Peter Dazeley. **163 Alamy Images:** MBI. **165 Alamy Images:** Blend Images. **167 Getty Images:** Radius Images. **168 Alamy Images:** nandana de silva. **170 Alamy Images:** Huntstock, Inc. **174 Alamy Images:** Janine Wiedel Photolibrar. **176 Shutterstock:** Yuri Arcurs. **178 Alamy Images:** / Mary Evans Picture Library. **180 Alamy Images:** Christina Kennedy. **182 Alamy Images:** Somos Images. **185 Alamy Images:** Juice Images. **186 Alamy Images:** Angela Hampton Picture Library. **190 Alamy Images:** Bubbles Photolibrary / Lucy Tizard. **192 Alamy Images:** Mike Abrahams. **195 Alamy Images:** Steven May. **196 Alamy Images:** MBI. **198 Alamy Images:** Moodboard. **201 Corbis:** Imagemore Co., Ltd. **202 Alamy Images:** Nick Gregory. **205 Corbis:** Hill Street Studios / Blend Images. **207 Alamy Images:** David J. Green - lifestyle 2. **208 Alamy Images:** Margit Mollenhauer. **210 Shutterstock:** Blaj Gabriel. **215 Getty Images:** Dorling Kindersley. **216 Getty Images:** Taxi / Manfred Rutz. **219 Alamy Images:** Image Source

Cover images: *Front:* **Getty Images:** Westend61; *Back:* **Alamy Images:** Juice Images r; **Shutterstock:** Monkey Business Images

All other images © Pearson Education

Introduction

Thank you for purchasing the BTEC Entry 3/Level 1 Health and Social Care Teaching Book and Resource Disk. This book and disk have been designed for you to use alongside the BTEC Entry 3/Level 1 Health and Social Care Student Book to help you and your learners through the most popular units of the specification.

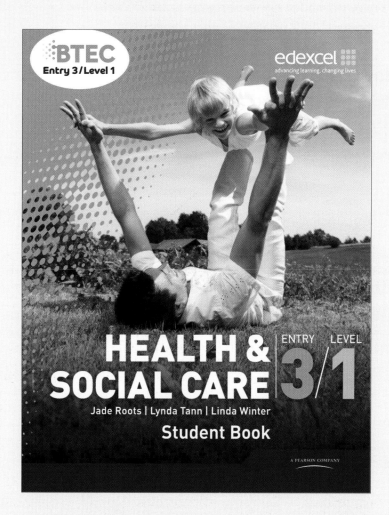

When delivering a BTEC qualification you become the examiner. The specification provides you with an outline of the unit content you should deliver. It also contains guidance about methods of delivery and assessment. However, you will design the assignments to assess your learners' achievements. The assignments should be appropriate for your learners. (All BTEC assignments must be verified by someone in your centre before they are issued to learners to ensure they are fit for purpose.)

Foundation Learning and BTEC Entry 3 and Level 1 Health and Social Care

Foundation Learning (FL) is the new name for provision and learning at Entry Level and Level 1 for all learners (14-19 year-olds and adults).

FL is replacing existing qualifications from E1 to L1 (excluding adult safeguarded learning). As of 2010 funding will not be available for Foundation Learning qualifications not accredited on the QCF.

Edexcel offers a complete programme of qualifications to fulfil the requirements of the FL framework, which covers three strands:

- Vocational learning

- Personal and social development (including BTEC WorkSkills)

- Functional skills.

BTEC Entry 3 and Level 1 Health and Social Care falls into the vocational strand of the curriculum, and would work within a broader FL curriculum. You'll notice in the tables that follow that the FL curriculum allows for a range of ability within different parts of the curriculum (e.g. functional skills at L1 and L2) allowing learners to really play to their strengths and develop their skills.

Example of a FL curriculum for an Entry 3 learner:

Edexcel BTEC Entry Level (Entry 3) Award in Health and Social Care	Entry 3	6 credits
Edexcel BTEC Entry Level Certificate in WorkSkills (PSD strand)	Entry 3	13 credits
Functional skills in Mathematics	Entry 3	5 credits
Functional skills in ICT	Entry 2	5 credits
Functional skills in English	Entry 3	5 credits
Full programme		34 credits
Approximate guided learning hours		340

Example of a FL curriculum for an Level 1 learner:

Edexcel BTEC Level 1 Certificate in Health and Social Care	Level 1	13 credits
Edexcel Entry Level Certificate in Personal and Social Development	Entry 2	13 credits
Edexcel BTEC Entry Level Award in WorkSkills	Entry 3	3 credits
Functional skills in Mathematics	Entry 3	5 credits
Functional skills in ICT	Level 1	5 credits
Functional skills in English	Level 3	5 credits
Full programme		44 credits
Approximate guided learning hours		440

About the Health and Social Care sector

The Health and Social Care sector forms an integral part of helping our society to function and perform in the United Kingdom. The NHS is in the top 5 of the biggest employers in the world providing a wide range of services. The Health and Social Care sector has a workforce of over 440,000 and countless more volunteers working in businesses and organisations throughout the UK spread across the public, private and voluntary sectors.

About your BTEC Entry 3/ Level 1 Health and Social Care

The BTEC Entry 3/Level 1 Health and Social Care qualification has been developed in the Health and Social Care sector to:

- give learners opportunities to achieve a nationally recognised Entry or Level 1 vocationally related qualification

- allow learners to progress to employment in the Health and Social Care sector

- allow learners to progress to a Level 2 vocational qualification, such as the BTEC Level 2 First in Health and Social Care

- give learners the opportunity to develop a range of skills, techniques, personal skills and attributes essential for successful performance in working life.

Structure of the BTEC Entry 3 and BTEC Level 1 Health and Social Care

The BTEC Entry 3/Level 1 Health and Social Care is made up of 24 units. There are no mandatory units or formal pathways in the structure, which gives you the flexibility to select units and build a programme that will best meet the requirements, needs and interests of your learners.

The rules of combination for BTEC Entry 3 and BTEC Level 1 Health and Social Care are shown below:

Edexcel BTEC Entry Level Award (Entry 3) in Health and Social Care
1. Qualification credit value: a minimum of 6 credits.
2. Minimum credit to be achieved at, or above, the level of the qualification: 4 credits.
3. All credits must be achieved from the units listed in the specification.
Edexcel BTEC Level 1 Award in Health and Social Care
1. Qualification credit value: a minimum of 7 credits.
2. Minimum credit to be achieved at, or above, the level of the qualification: 4 credits.
3. All credits must be achieved from the units listed in the specification.

Edexcel BTEC Level 1 Certificate in Health and Social Care
1. Qualification credit value: a minimum of 13 credits.
2. Minimum credit to be achieved at, or above, the level of the qualification: 7 credits.
3. All credits must be achieved from the units listed in the specification.
Edexcel BTEC Level 1 Diploma in Health and Social Care
1. Qualification credit value: a minimum of 37 credits.
2. Minimum credit to be achieved at, or above, the level of the qualification: 20 credits.
3. All credits must be achieved from the units listed in the specification.
*Award and certificate credit boundaries may show slight variance for certain sectors.

Delivery

The Edexcel BTEC Entry 3/Level 1 Health and Social Care resources cover a selection of the most popular units for the sector, including two WorkSkills units, to make it easy for you to plan course delivery.

For extra support for WorkSkills units falling within the Entry 3 and Level 1 qualifications, but not covered in these resources, Edexcel offer further resources: the WorkSkills Activator workbooks (at Level 1 and Level 2; 9781846903366 / 9781846903359) and Teacher Resource Disk (Level 1 and 2; 9781846903373).

Many modes of delivery can be used for BTEC. The Resource Disk that accompanies this book provides a wealth of supporting material for your sector.

Functional skills

Your learners might be taking their BTEC alongside Functional Skills, particularly if they are taking BTEC to fulfil the vocational requirement of the Foundation Learning framework.

These qualifications in English, Mathematics and ICT are all about being able to apply learning in context and so provide a natural link to BTEC Entry 3 and Level Health and Social Care.

The BTEC Entry 3/Level 1 Health and Social Care gives your learners opportunities to develop functional skills within a sector-related context. You will find relevant functional skills highlighting which skills can be targeted by activities. Please note, this is not definitive; each activity gives learners the opportunity to develop and demonstrate many skills. All of the functional skills and the requirements of each specific skill are also mapped and covered in further detail in Annexe E of the BTEC Entry 3 and Level 1 Health and Social Care Specification.

Working with local employers

Employability skills are a key focus in BTEC Entry 3 and Level 1 Health and Social Care. One of the best ways for learners to get to grips with the learning and assessment required for this part of the course is to try their hand at the real thing.

A good way of giving learners hands on experience is to arrange a work placement in a health and social care setting. Good placements include residential/ nursing homes, nurseries, play groups and day care centres.

Learners could attend for a block placement for example a week, or attend 1 day a week for a period of time (for example, every Monday for half a term).

Learners should be given a list of qualities, jobs, and tasks that they should aim to achieve whilst they are on their placement which could be ticked off by the placement supervisor.

Learners should also be visited whilst they are on their placement to show support to the learner and also the placement.

Learners will also need to fully CRB checked to ensure they are safe to work with vulnerable groups.

Where placements are not available or suitable, guest speakers could be arranged from local health and social care settings to give learners an insight into their roles.

Assessment

BTECs are assessed by a series of assignments that you set. Learners will complete them throughout their course, either individually or in groups. For guidance on how to design BTEC assignments refer to www.btec.co.uk and to the guidance in your specification.

In the BTEC Entry Level and Level 1 qualifications all units are internally assessed. Each centre must register a Lead Internal Verifier to lead this process. They need to be assessed through Edexcel's online standardisation system (OSCA2). For more information on completing OSCA2. see the Edexcel website.

Collecting assessment evidence

Evidence for assessment may be generated through a range of activities including performance observation, presentations and posters. Learners should be encouraged to take responsibility for their own learning and achievement, taking into account industry standards for behaviour and performance. Evidence submitted by learners for the assessment needs to adhere to your internal verification process.

Each unit covered in these resources ends with an assessment overview page. This helps your learners track what they need to achieve in each unit, and where they can find the information to help them do so, plus invaluable tips from BTEC experts on improving assignment success.

Grading

Learners are required to satisfy *all* the assessment criteria in a unit to pass each unit. Qualifications are graded as pass or fail.

How to use this Teaching Book and Resource Disk

This Teaching Book contains the information you need to deliver the course, combining engaging content coverage with hands-on activities and tips for learners. It is designed to work in conjunction with the Student Book for this sector, supplementing the content found there with delivery support which can be found on the accompanying Resource Disk.

The book covers a broad range of both Entry 3 and Level 1 units to allow you maximum freedom in course design and broad support for delivery.

This material is repeated here in your Teaching Book, so you have all your teaching resources in one place. See Student Book pp. vi–viii for information on page features used to make learning easier for your learners.

As there is overlap between some of the content across Entry Level and Level 1 units in this qualification, we have ensured that the material provided can be used to deliver the Entry Level unit only, if this is what is required for your learners.

The Teacher Resource Disk maps out the related Entry Level Learning Outcomes in the Scheme of Work and the Assessment Criteria in the Assessment grid, for the following Level 1 units:

L1 Unit 8 – links to Unit 1 Investigating Rights and Responsibilities at Work

L1 Unit 9 – links to Unit 2 Managing Your Health at Work

L1 Unit 12 – links to E3 Unit 5 Health Needs

L1 Unit 14 – links to E3 Unit 6 Introduction to Creative and Leisure Activities for Children and Adults

L1 Unit 16 – links to E3 Unit 6 Introduction to Creative and Leisure Activities for Children and Adults

L1 Unit 17 – links to E3 Unit 7 The Role of the Carer at Mealtimes

How to use the CD-ROM

You'll find a copy of the accompanying Resource Disk CD-ROM attached to the book.

This stand-alone CD-ROM contains a supporting file full of delivery support for each unit including the following:

- An introduction – outlines the key learning outcomes of the unit and content covered.

- A scheme of work – provides guidance on how to combine the Student Book and Teacher Disk resources to help you create interesting lessons. Schemes of work do not use guided learning hours as these are not part of delivery at this level. Instead they provide suggested learning time based on qualification specification guidance.

- Delivery guidance – provides guidance on delivering the course, including tips on interesting activities, integrating functional skills and making the course practical.

- An assessment grid – maps the assessment criteria for that unit to the activities that support them in the Student Book, as well as suggesting forms of evidence.

Lesson plan

The lesson plan below gives you an example of the innovative and creative ways you can deliver the course using Edexcel's BTEC Entry 3/ Level 1 resources.

This is a 2 hour lesson.

Week: 1

Unit 19: Job opportunities in Health and Social care

LO1: Know about different types of career opportunities available in Health and Social Care

Aim: To be able to describe and compare two different job roles within Health and Social Care. One should be a direct care role such as a nurse the other should be an indirect care role such as a health/dental technician.

Timing	Tutor activity	Learner activity	Resources
5 mins	Tutor introduces aims and objectives for lesson and explains use of learner diary	Learners note down aims and objective in learner diary	Learning objective and assessment criteria as listed in Unit 19 Student Book, p.185
20 mins	Tutor splits learners into small groups. Tutor explains the difference between direct and indirect care Groups to look at job roles in: • Direct Care • Indirect Care	Each group of learners asked to think of as many different job roles as possible under these categories and to identify the main similarities and differences. For example, they should look at the amount of time spent with clients and what each job role is responsible for. They should develop a series of questions to use with a representative from the job role and answer skills to be developed for English functional skills.	Tutor should provide website references and a connexions representative could be brought in for a question and answer session on job roles. Learners should also be encouraged to download job descriptions / advertisements from websites such as NHS direct. Learner diaries to record their ideas at the end of the session. (Learners should cover both job role areas and if possible examples of areas that the employees are responsible for. They could also annotate them with their own thoughts).
15 mins	Tutor to lead feedback session by making notes of information from learners on board	Learners to appoint speaker for each group to feedback and all learners to contribute to discussion.	Student Book for further information on each career area. Computer Job centre leaflets collected by learners before start of unit as homework

30 mins	Explanation of the direct and indirect care roles in Health and social care Tutor to lead discussion on the difference between a skill and a quality Tutor to select two examples one from each area and discuss how their roles differ and the different skills and qualities they will need	Discuss the ways in which direct careers and indirect career job roles differ Use internet to research areas of employment and carry out first case study task	Student Book for further information on each career area and related activities/case studies for supporting understanding of direct and indirect careers
20 mins	Tutor to develop understanding of different skills and qualities needed to work in direct and indirect care sector by asking learners to identify their own skills and qualities	Learners to identify their own skills and qualities Learners to carry out activities based on case studies about skills and qualities needed for both areas of employment	Internet access, employment leaflets Learner diary
10 mins	Individual or group research based on activity on page 187 Tutor should identify key points from activity such as job description and main points of responsibility	Learners to draw up table to show findings of further research (use IT as part of functional skills)	Internet access, learner diary for notes
10 mins	Learners should now be encouraged to read through notes and the tutor should make sure that they can describe and compare the two job roles. The tutor should have a one to one dialogue to check through each learners notes to ensure they cover key points.	Learners to start to type up any appropriate work to demonstrate functional skills in IT. They should make sure that the key points are identified and have an explanation of at least 2 different contrasts and similarities. Learners could be encouraged to use a double bubble diagram to support the process.	Computer, learner diary
5 mins	Knowledge Check	Q and A session	

INVESTIGATING RIGHTS & RESPONSIBILITIES AT WORK

Everyone has the right to get a job, receive medical treatment, go shopping, have an education and travel freely. What we often forget is that we have a right to do these things safely without fear of being bullied, called names or assaulted.

In the United Kingdom we have lots of rights. For example everyone has the right to an education, or if you are at work you have the right to be paid money. Sometimes it is our responsibility to help people to know what a right is and to understand what rights they have. When you are in the workplace you will be expected to reinforce and respect the rights of others, and understand that you as an employee have rights as well as your employer.

In this unit you will:

● Learn about what rights and responsibilities you have

● Find out about how to respect the rights of others

● Look at laws that can protect you at work

● Find out what responsibilities employers have

Does everyone have the right to work in health and social care?

L01 Our basic human rights

We all have **rights** when receiving health and social care and these rights influence the way we are treated. We all have what are known as '**human rights**'. What human rights do you think we have?

The right to life

Your life is protected by the law, which means that no one is allowed to harm you and in return you are not allowed to harm other people. Your life and the lives of others are all important and worthwhile.

The right to an education

We are lucky in the United Kingdom as everyone is allowed to go to school or college to learn. Education means you can have a better life and get a job. Unfortunately in other countries, there are some groups of people, especially women, who are not allowed an education.

The right to freedom of thought

Everyone has the right to hold opinions and say their views. You may have a broad range of views, beliefs and thoughts, including a religious faith. Although you have a right to express these thoughts, you have to remember that other people also have a right not to be **discriminated** against.

* **Key terms**

Rights
Something we are allowed to have by law.

Human rights
Basic rights and freedoms, which all humans are allowed.

Discriminate
Treating someone unfairly because of their beliefs, gender, sexuality, age or ethnicity.

Respect
Valuing an individual or a decision they have made.

Everyone has the right to make a peaceful protest

The right to be treated with respect and dignity

In a health and social care setting, any user of the service wants to be treated with **respect** and dignity. Treating people with respect and dignity could range from saying 'Please' or 'Thank you' to asking the user of the service what they would like to eat for dinner.

Activity: Your rights

We are lucky to live in a country that gives us so many rights.

1. What rights do we have? List as many as you can think of.

2. Compare your ideas with others in the class. Add any that you do not have to your list.

3. Using your list of rights, make a leaflet that informs users of health and social care services of their basic rights. Give some information about each right. Try to include a small description of at least three human rights.

Tip: Think about: What is the right? What does it do? What is its purpose? How does it protect us?

Check

- Rights can influence the way that we are treated

- We are all entitled to human rights

- It is up to you to promote an individual's rights in health and social care settings.

L01 Rights at work

When you have a job it is important that you are treated fairly at work and that you treat other workers fairly too.

Healthy and safe environment

When you are at work you will notice that your **employer** will have made some rules about health and safety to make sure that you and others are kept safe in the work **environment**. Your manager will make the rules, but it is up to you to follow them.

Working conditions

Different kinds of jobs have different kinds of **working conditions**. If you are working in a nursery, then you will work from around 8.30am–4.00pm Monday to Friday, spending all day with children. However, if you are a carer in a nursing home you may be expected to work longer shifts, including nights.

Key working conditions

Make sure that you do not work more than 48 hours per week, and you have a 20-minute break every six hours.

Washing your hands is vital before food preparation.

Privacy of personal information

Your workplace is not allowed to give out any of your **personal information** to anyone (even if you know them) unless you agree to it. You are not allowed to give out anyone's personal details, unless they agree to it.

Fair pay/wages and paid holiday time

Whatever your gender, age or appearance, you should be paid fairly. No matter what job you have, it is the law that your employer gives you some time away from work every year (**holiday time**) and pays you for it.

✳ Key terms

Environment
The setting you are in.

Employer
A person who pays workers to do jobs for them. Can also be known as the manager or the owner.

Working conditions
The basic rights you have at work.

Personal information
Details about you, such as your name, address, telephone number and email address.

Holiday time
Paid time off work.

❗ Remember

When making a snack, remember to:

- Wash your hands before you start
- Use clean utensils
- Make sure the food is not past its 'Best before' date
- Clean up after yourself.

Case study:
Should men and women be treated differently at work?

Glen and Jane have just started work as carers at Stones Residential Home. Petrina is their employer. Petrina has told Glen and Jane that they will get paid differently because Glen is a man and Jane is a woman. Glen has also been told to work 12 hour shifts with only a 10 minute break, whereas Jane only has to work eight-hour shifts and gets two hours off. Petrina says it is because 'Men are more able to cope with the long hours'. Glen and Jane are sure that this isn't correct, but do not know their rights.

1. **Should Jane and Glen be paid differently because of their gender?**
2. **Is it fair that Glen is working longer hours with shorter breaks than Jane?**
3. **What is Petrina doing wrong? What should she do?**
4. **What advice would you give Glen and Jane?**

Activity: Being a manager of a day care centre

Noshin is training to be the manager of a **day care centre**, but she keeps leaving personal details of the users of the service lying around the centre. She also forgets to wash her hands before making the food, and has told her **employees** that if they have a day off, she will not pay them.

1. Working in pairs, think of three key pieces of advice you would give Noshin.
2. Role-play what you would say to her, with one of you playing Noshin.
3. Discuss as a class what rights Noshin is breaking.

Key terms

Day care centre
A setting usually for older people or people with learning difficulties and disabilities to help maintain independence and provide companionship.

Employee
Someone who works for a company or organisation.

Check

- Everyone has rights at work
- Employers must respect the rights of workers
- Some employees don't know about their rights as workers and are mistreated as a result.

L01 Responsibilities

Every job will have lots of everyday tasks and **responsibilities** that are only related to that job in the health and social care setting where the job is being practised. For example, the responsibilities of staff working at a day centre for people with disabilities are big and involve more than just making cups of tea for the **users of the service**.

What responsibilities do you think a nursery worker would have?

Responsibility to protect

When you use a health and social care service like a nursery or a hospital, you trust the staff to look after you. You do not expect a child to go to nursery and come home with food poisoning because the kitchen is not clean.

Therefore it is your responsibility when working in a health and social care setting to protect the users of the service.

Work responsibilities

It is important when you start a new job that you understand exactly what your manager will expect you to do every day. This can normally be found in your contract. You will be asked to sign a contract before you start work.

If you do not carry out your daily tasks properly, you will be breaking your contract and you may risk losing your job.

As well as following your contract, you have to follow health and safety rules, which are there to keep you safe at work.

Activity: Sources of help and advice

You may need to seek advice on rights and responsibilities at various times when you are working in a health and social care setting. In pairs, think about the various places where you could find sources of support in the workplace.

✳ Key terms

Responsibility
When someone is trusted to carry out a job or task.

User of service
Anyone who uses health and social care services, such as a hospital patient, a child going to school or an elderly resident in a nursing home.

! Remember

When carrying out the day-to-day tasks of a carer in a residential home, remember to:

- Put clean sheets on the residents' beds
- Bath the residents
- Help the residents to get dressed
- Make the dinner
- Provide recreational activities for the residents.

What would happen if the carers didn't complete their daily tasks?

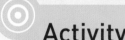

Activity: You decide

You are the manager of a health centre which contains a dentist, doctor's surgery, children's nursery and a main reception. You need to employ the following staff:

- A dentist
- A nurse
- A nursery worker
- A receptionist
- A cleaner.

Choose two staff from the list above and write an advert for a newspaper advertising the jobs. The advert should give a general description of what each job involves.

Functional skills

By producing a newspaper advert, you will be demonstrating your English writing skills.

Check

- Employers and employees have responsibilities in a health and social care setting, to each other and users of the service

- The responsibilities of your job are normally laid out in a contract, which you sign when you start your job

- If you do not carry out your responsibilities, you could be asked to leave your job.

L02 Factors affecting rights of individuals

Everyone wants to live in a society that treats everyone equally and fairly. However, some people are discriminated against, for instance because of their gender, their age or where they come from.

Discrimination

Our society is unequal and some people feel that they do not get the same chances as others. For example, they may be treated differently because of their name, age, skin colour or where they live. The word 'discrimination' is used when people are not being treated fairly.

Stereotyping

Stereotyping people is something that we should try to avoid. We know that all people are individuals; they like different music, have different hobbies and eat different food.

You may have heard people refer to particular groups of individuals in certain ways, for example, 'girls can't play football' or 'teenagers are thugs'.

Stereotypes can also be positive. Can you think of any positive stereotypes?

Negative stereotypes of particular groups of people can make us act differently towards them. This can lead to discrimination.

* **Key terms**

Factors
Things that can influence or affect us.

Stereotyping
When society makes assumptions about an individual or group of people.

Groups of people are often negatively stereotyped

Activity: Stereotypes

List as many stereotypes as you can for the following groups and think of how this could affect them in a negative way:

- Children
- Teenagers
- Older people
- Adults.

Cultural background

Everyone has a different **culture**. You might have to help do some household chores around your home or you may be expected to have a part-time job, whereas your friends might not have to do any chores at all. In some cultures, you may be expected to attend a place of worship or dress in a particular way. Differences in culture can cause some people to be treated unfairly by others.

✳ Key term

Culture
The rules we follow, the manners we have and the way we live.

Case study:
Kamill

Kamill has been working as a hospital porter for four years and has always received praise from the hospital patients he has helped. Kamill wears a turban as part of his religion and it has never been a problem. Recently, a new manager has started working with Kamill. He has told Kamill that he cannot wear his turban at work as it is not part of the hospital uniform.

1. Should Kamill have to remove his turban at work?

2. How does this discrimination affect Kamill's rights?

3. What advice would you give to Kamill?

Activity: Group discussion

1. Take a few minutes to think about whether you would rather be a male or a female. Why? Try to write your answer down.

2. Discuss your answer with other people in the class. Who would they rather be? Why?

Check

- Some people are treated unfairly by others because of their differences
- Stereotyping is grouping people together and saying they all are one thing, it can lead to discrimination
- It is important to remember that not everyone will share our values and opinions.

L02 Respecting others

Treating others with respect and courtesy helps everyone work well together. Your classmates, workmates and users of the service need to be treated with respect so that they will feel welcome.

Appropriate behaviour

Everyone likes to enjoy themselves and have a good time, but there are certain times when you may need to moderate your behaviour or change it completely. Some people use swear words as a way to express themselves, but when you are working with people, particularly children, it is very important that you don't swear as children may copy you.

There will also be times when you will have to be polite to people you are communicating with. This could be when looking after adults, or talking to users of the service or their family. It is important to be polite as this will help to make the user of the service feel more welcome.

Behaviour in the workplace

While you are at work, you must do what your employer tells you to do. You must do the task as soon as they ask you (even if you disagree) as putting it off could put someone in danger, or could mean that you discriminate against someone without realising it.

It is important to understand that everyone is different and may have different likes and dislikes from you. By understanding these differences, you can help a person to feel comfortable in the setting.

Why is it important to clean up after you have used an area?

Case study:

Tabatha and Marley

Tabatha and Marley have both started a week's trial working at a children's nursery. Only one person can get the job. Tabatha is getting on really well. She is polite to the parents and children when they arrive, she listens to the children and tidies up when she has played with them. The parents and staff like Tabatha.

However, several parents have complained that their children have started using swear words and Marley has been heard swearing in front of the children. Marley only likes to play with the boys but can be quite lively and likes to throw glitter, paint and toys around. Marley doesn't tidy up; she just moves onto the next activity. Some staff are annoyed as some equipment has been found broken after Marley has used it.

1. **Who would you give the job to? Why?**
2. **What was wrong with Marley swearing in front of the children?**
3. **How did Tabatha behave?**
4. **What did Marley do wrong?**
5. **What would you tell Marley to do differently?**

✓ Check

- People need to be treated with respect to feel welcome and safe
- It is good to be polite in the workplace
- Think about what behaviour is appropriate for the health and social care setting you are in
- Follow your manager's instructions.

! Remember

When working in a health and social care setting, remember to:

- Be polite
- Clear up after yourself
- Speak to all users of the service (not just the ones you like)
- Don't swear
- Follow your manager's instructions.

L03 Laws that protect you at work

There are laws and regulations to ensure that employees are safe and treated fairly and equally at work. Different workplaces will also have their own **policies** (guidelines) to make sure the setting is a safe place for everyone. The laws are also there to protect other workers as well as the users of the services.

Health and Safety Act (1974)

This is an important law which is designed to protect everyone in the workplace. It also makes employees responsible for their own safety as well as the safety of others.

Under this law:

* Employees must use the health and safety equipment provided, e.g. disposable gloves
* Employees must report any accidents, hazards or dangers, e.g. tell your manager if you see a broken toy.

Data Protection Act (1998)

This law protects people's rights to confidentiality of personal information. It means that personal and private information is kept safe and cannot be accessed by others. This applies to:

* Personal information being discussed, e.g. giving out your address to someone over the phone
* Written information that is personal, e.g. a child's family background
* Electronic records, e.g. a person's medical history.

Race Relations Act (2000), Sex Discrimination Act (1975), Disability Discrimination Act (2005)

These three laws aim to ensure that people are not discriminated against because of their:

* Religion
* Ethnicity
* Sex or gender
* Disability.

> **✳ Key term**
>
> **Policy**
> A guideline that tells you what to do in given situations.

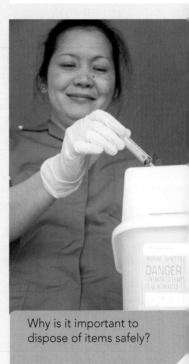

Why is it important to dispose of items safely?

These laws make it illegal to treat people unfairly just because they are different from you. The laws protect people at work, at school or college, when looking for a job, using public transport, finding somewhere to live or receiving medical treatment.

Activity: Tell us the law

You have been asked to make a poster that tells employees of the different laws that protect them while they are at work. Make sure your poster includes a little information about each law and try to make it colourful and interesting.

Employer's responsibilities

Your employer is responsible for treating you fairly. To make sure that this happens, your working conditions will be written in a contract. When you sign the contract, you are agreeing to these conditions. When you start a new job, make sure that your employer gives you a contract and that you read it first; this way you can discuss anything you are not happy with before you agree to the working conditions.

Check

- Employers and employees have to follow laws to make sure that they and users of the service are kept safe and treated fairly

- By not following these rules, you are breaking the law and could be fined or sent to prison

- There are lots of laws to be aware of

- Workplaces will have policies based on the law, telling you what to do in certain situations.

L04 Equality of opportunity

We all want others to treat us fairly and with respect. We want to be given the same chances as others and get help when needed. People have a right to be treated fairly no matter what the colour of their skin, their physical appearance, their background, culture, religion, and so on.

Responsibilities of the workplace

It is up to your employer to make sure that all staff and users of the service feel safe and comfortable. This means that staff and other users of the service do not discriminate against each other and that all staff follow the laws that were made to protect everyone.

Equality of opportunity means making sure that every user of the service and member of staff is treated fairly. It does not mean treating everyone the same. This would not help those who need specialist equipment or extra help and support.

Your employer will want to show staff and users of the service that they treat everyone equally, no matter who they are. They might do this by having posters around the setting showing people of different ages, abilities and disabilities, gender and **ethnicity**. They might provide a range of different foods in the canteen, such as vegetarian options. What else could they do?

> *** Key term**
>
> **Ethnicity**
> Belonging to a group that shares many characteristics. These characteristics can be different from other ethnicities.

It is important to show that everyone is welcome and treated equally

Activity: What would you do?

Look at the following examples and think about how the individuals might feel. What should the employers and employees do differently?

1. The nursery is making Mother's Day cards. Austin lives in a children's home. He is told not to bother making one.

2. The residential home is making a beef roast dinner for all the residents. Tina is vegetarian but is told that she will have to eat the dinner as they are treating everyone the same.

3. Sarah only has the use of one arm. She is told that there is no point in trying to play netball.

4. Rashid receives a letter from his doctor but cannot read it as he does not speak English.

Check

- There are several groups of people that are discriminated against in our society

- Employers must make sure that employees are given equal opportunities at work

- Employees must make sure that users of the service are given equal opportunities to use the service

- Promoting equal opportunities does not mean treating everyone the same.

L04 Confidentiality

In health and social care settings, people who work with **vulnerable** individuals will find out a lot of information about the individual and their needs. This information is useful because it helps the provider of the service to meet the individual's needs. For example, a child might be sad because her mother and father are splitting up; if workers know the reason, they can respond well to the child.

However, you may find out information about the users of the service, their families, or even other members of staff, which they do not want other people to know. This information is **confidential** and must not be passed on.

Your employer also has a responsibility to keep certain information about you, or any other employee, as well as the company or workplace itself, confidential.

Sometimes you may have to tell a more senior worker or manager about information you receive, for example when you believe that a person is at risk or in danger. This is the only time when you should pass on confidential information.

Key terms

Vulnerable
When an individual is at risk of harm.

Confidential
Keeping information secret.

! Remember

When working in a health and social care office, remember to:

- Put files about the users of the service away
- Put password controls on computers
- Lock the door to the office.

Case study:

Clare and Kirsty

Clare and her friend, Kirsty, are waiting to see the **physiotherapist** at the local health centre when two staff come in, talking loudly about one of their clients. Clare knows the client they are talking about – Ozzy who is their neighbour. The staff talk about Ozzy's personal hygiene. They are now standing next to Clare and Kirsty, and although Clare 'coughs' to let them know they are there, the staff members keep on talking.

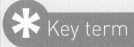

Key term

Physiotherapist
Professional who helps individuals gain use of particular body movements.

Activity: Group discussion

1. Should the staff be talking about Ozzy?

2. If so, where should they be talking about him?

3. How do you think Clare and Kirsty felt about hearing the staff talk about Ozzy?

4. Might their opinion of Ozzy change?

5. Do you think Clare and Kirsty might act differently towards Ozzy?

Activity: What's the problem?

Look at the cartoon of an office in a health and social care setting below.

1. Find five **breaches of confidentiality** in the cartoon.

2. With a partner discuss what you would do about each of the five breaches if you were the employer.

* Key term

Breach of confidentiality
Leaving information available for unauthorised people to see, or informing individuals of information when they do not need to know it.

Check

- Users of services rely on the providers of the service to keep them safe

- Information that is learnt about a user of the service is usually kept confidential

- Breaking confidentiality is the same as breaking someone's trust in you

- Always check whether you can pass the information on if you are unsure.

ASSESSMENT OVERVIEW

While working through this unit, you will have prepared for completing the following assessment tasks:

◯	1.1 Explain what 'rights' are	Pages 2–5
◯	1.2 Explain what 'responsibilities' are	Page 6–7
◯	2.1 Explain the factors that may affect the rights of individuals	Pages 8–9
◯	2.2 Explain how to respect the rights of individuals	Page 10–11
◯	3.1 Identify laws that can protect employee rights	Pages 12–13
◯	4.1 Identify employer responsibilities in regard to: • fulfilling a contract • health and safety • equal opportunities and prevention of discrimination	Pages 14–17

Assignment tips

- To help you pass this unit, produce a poster with pictures and titles of a number of rights and responsibilities, explaining what they are and giving examples. Make sure you cover both rights and responsibilities.

- Look at different case studies of people or carry out interviews to find out what factors have affected their rights and the way they have been treated.

- To show your understanding of the laws that keep us safe and treated fairly at work, create an information booklet or prepare a presentation to inform other people. The booklet must show how an employer should treat you.

MANAGING YOUR HEALTH AT WORK

Every year thousands of people are injured in the workplace. This is because some of the day-to-day tasks that you might have to carry out within your job role could cause you injuries or strains. For example, someone is more likely to suffer from a back injury if their job involves lifting and bending regularly.

This unit introduces you to several different areas of work and investigates the health requirements of the people working within these areas. It also explores health risks in detail and looks at ways in which injuries at work can be reduced.

In this unit you will:

- Learn about the different health requirements for employees in different places of work

- Know about the health risks involved in different areas of work

- Explain how to reduce health risks in different areas of work

Is this a safe way to lift a heavy box?

BTEC

L01 Health requirements in office-based & outdoor work

People work in a variety of places. Here are some examples.

Office-based work

Office-based work is usually carried out indoors by people sitting for long periods of time at desks in offices. Offices are rooms that can be very different in size – some may be very small whereas others might be quite large. Office staff usually have their own desk and chair to work from, but they may have to share other pieces of equipment, for example:

- Telephones

- Computers

- Fax machines

- Photocopiers.

Office work does not usually involve being very active or physical, but it can be mentally tiring as office workers have to think and concentrate a lot. Office workers' duties often include using computers, communicating with others and keeping records and files.

Outdoor work

Construction industry

The construction industry designs, builds and improves buildings and the surrounding areas. This area of work can be carried out indoors or outdoors and the people that work in this area can be expected to work in several different places.

Construction workers have to be fit as a lot of their job involves being on their feet for long periods of time. Their work may involve lifting and moving things and they need to be fit enough to do this. Some construction workers have to use heavy equipment during their working day and may have to drive large trucks and lorries.

Why is it important for this bricklayer to be fit and in good health?

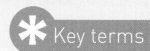

Gardening

Gardeners usually work outdoors, growing and looking after plants, flowers, grass and vegetables. They work in different types of weather and in different places, including **rural** and **urban** areas.

During their working day gardeners have lots of fresh air. However, some work indoors in glasshouses or greenhouses, which can be very hot and stuffy.

Farming

Farms are areas of land that are usually used to grow certain **crops** that can be sold for food. Some farms breed and rear animals which can also be used for food purposes. People who work on farms spend much of their working day outdoors. Farmers work long hours and some of the work they have to do can be very physical.

Activity: Who works where?

Working in pairs, make a list of all the different jobs that you think people do in each of the following areas:

- Offices

- Construction industry

- Gardening

- Farming.

Check

- Office-based work is mentally demanding

- Outdoor work is physically demanding

- People who work outside have to work in lots of different weathers.

L01 Health requirements in the service industry

The service industry provides services, doing things for people, not goods, providing things for people.

Hospitals

Hospitals are places where people go to receive health care. Some people go to a hospital as an outpatient – their treatment, diagnosis or therapy is completed on the same day. Other people go as an inpatient – they have to stay in hospital and have the treatment overnight.

Many hospitals have lots of different departments offering several types of treatment to their patients, for example:

- Accident and emergency – provides urgent treatment for accidents or illnesses

- Maternity services – looks after women in pregnancy and during and after having a baby

- Paediatrics – provides care and treatment for sick and injured children

- Orthopaedics – looks after people who have problems with their bones, joints and muscles

- General wards – rooms where people stay to rest and get better

- Operating theatres – places where surgeons repair damage to part of a person's body

- Pharmacy – hands out medicines.

Hospital work can be both physically and mentally tiring, as carers quite often have several patients to care for at any one time. Also, they are on their feet for long periods and need to concentrate on the care that they deliver to their patients.

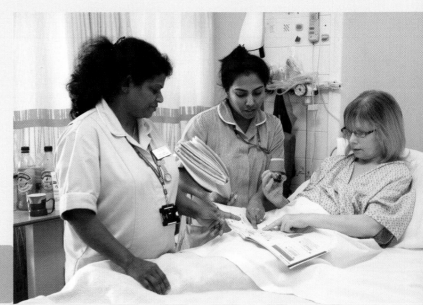

Nurses attending to one of their many patients

Care homes

These are places where people can go to live when they need help with their daily living tasks. Care homes are generally used by older people, however individuals with disabilities might also stay in a care home. Care homes usually offer comfortable surroundings in a safe and secure environment that feels quite similar to that of the service user's own home.

Childcare

There are various places that provide childcare. Here are some examples:

Person's own home	Usually delivered by a child minder. This type of care is useful for working parents who want to leave their child in a familiar environment.
Playschool/preschool	Place where children usually go when they are almost three years old. Playschools/preschools are sometimes held in local community halls or can be attached to a local infant school. A number of children will go to the same playschool/preschool and they will be of mixed ages, usually between two and five.
Nursery	Similar to playschools, nurseries provide education for very young children before they go to full-time school.
Crèche	Place where children can go to be looked after while their main carers are busy or at work.
Infant school	Usually run and funded by the government to provide an education for children between the ages of four and seven. They are held in purpose-built buildings that are usually designed for the local community.

Activity: Areas of work in hospitals

Produce a leaflet that shows different areas of work within a hospital. Remember to use pictures and colour to make your leaflet eye-catching.

Functional skills

By producing a leaflet, you will be demonstrating your English writing skills.

Check

- Care services are provided for people of all ages
- All forms of care are physically demanding.

L01 Health requirements in retail, public services & sport & leisure

Retail

People who work in the retail industry usually work in shops, selling goods to the general public. Most of them will work indoors in buildings that can be of very different sizes. The size of the building will also depend on the size of the **organisation** that owns the shop; for example, a department store that sells lots of different goods and employs many staff over several floors, or a small corner shop that employs just a few people. However, goods can also be sold on market stalls, which means a person's area of work can be outdoors.

Public services

Fire service

The fire service is provided by the government to mainly deal with emergencies involving fires. However, a firefighter is also trained on how to rescue people from dangerous buildings and how to free people from car crashes. Firefighters work in some very dangerous situations and can be involved in circumstances that may be stressful and upsetting.

Police

The police are people who work for the government to help keep law and order. They spend a lot of their time preventing and detecting crimes and have powers that they can use to stop people from behaving in a way that might cause harm or injury to other people or their property. Police officers often work in very stressful situations and have to deal with many different types of people in their day-to-day duties.

Key terms

Organisation
A company or place of work.

Public services
Services provided by the government for its people, e.g. fire service, police.

What health risks does this firefighter face?

Sport and leisure

The sport and leisure industry is made up of several different types of establishment. Most are privately run and are organisations that are set up to make a profit from their clients. Here are some examples of sport and leisure establishments:

Gym	A place where people can do physical exercise
Leisure centre	A place that provides leisure facilities, such as sports halls, meeting rooms and cafés
Park	An area of land that the general public can use for leisure and recreational activities
Swimming pool	A man-made area of water where people can swim and play
Tennis club	A place where people can learn and play tennis, usually privately owned and run
Football club	Privately or community-run club which teaches and plays football
Ice skating rink	Indoor or outdoor facilities that enable people to get exercise while gliding on ice
Spa centre	A place where you can relax and have treatments such as facials and massages

Activity: What's in your area?

1. How many different sports and leisure facilities are there in your area?

2. What types of thing does each facility provide?

Check

- The retail industry is concerned with selling goods to the general public

- Public services provided by the government are there to help protect you and keep you safe

- Some public services are provided by the private sector.

L01 Health requirements

It is important to be healthy at work, this can benefit both you and your employer:

Many job roles come with expected health requirements. This means that your health and/or fitness must be of a certain standard for you to be able to perform some job roles in health and social care settings. This is because you will quite often be in contact with people with illnesses and you will need to be healthy enough not to catch them. Also, some job roles within the health and social care sector are physically demanding and you will need to be physically fit enough to cope with the demands of the job.

Hygiene

Good **hygiene** is essential in everyone's lives.

Good hygiene in the environment

This is to do with how clean people's surroundings are. Good environmental hygiene reduces the spread of infection and makes the surroundings look and smell nice.

Good personal hygiene

This is to do with how clean people's bodies are. It is important that you have good personal hygiene, as it makes you look professional and encourages good working relationships with your **colleagues** and clients.

Lifting weights

Lifting loads can be a serious hazard to a person's health and wellbeing and it is important that you are fit enough to carry out any tasks that may involve lifting. All care workers should have training in correct lifting techniques, and should be supplied with suitable equipment that helps to make lifting and moving things around much easier. This will help to keep employees healthy and will reduce the likelihood of injuries as a result of poor lifting techniques.

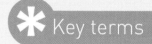

Key terms

Hygiene
Maintaining high levels of cleanliness at all times to prevent the spread of disease.

Colleague
A person that you work with.

Infection control

Infections can easily be passed from one person to another and it is important that you do everything you can to avoid passing infections on. Ways to control infections include:

- Practise good hand washing
- Wear protective clothing
- Clean up spillages immediately
- Don't share equipment
- Dispose of body waste correctly
- Sterilise equipment correctly
- Use correct barrier nursing methods.

Protective clothing

All health and social care workers are expected to use the correct personal protective equipment (PPE) when performing their job roles. Protective clothing helps reduce the risk of injury to the worker and can also help reduce the spread of infections. Examples of protective clothing used in health and social care settings include:

- Uniforms
- Disposable aprons
- Disposable gloves
- Disposable overshoes
- Disposable hats
- Hard hats
- Hairnets
- Face masks
- Safety shoes
- Goggles/safety glasses.

Key term

Infection
Disease caused by germs.

A nurse using appropriate PPE

Activity: How should I wash my hands?

Julie has just started work as a carer at Bluebell Nursing Home. She has not worked in a care home before and needs information on the procedures involved in effective hand washing.

Make a small poster or leaflet telling Julie how to wash her hands correctly. Don't forget to use pictures and colour.

Functional skills

By making a poster or leaflet, you will be demonstrating your English writing skills.

Check

- You must be in good health to work in health and social care settings
- Everyone must follow correct lifting techniques
- Protective clothing and equipment is provided to help keep you safe.

L01 More health requirements

Influence of the weather

The weather can have a huge impact on workers whose job roles involve outdoor work. Outdoor workers have to brave different weather conditions including the cold, rain, wind, snow and hail during the winter and autumn months, and the sun and heat in the summer and spring.

Outdoor elements

When working outdoors, workers have to consider the weather and the impact it can have on their job role. During the summer time, workers might be working in the sunshine and they need to ensure they do not get sunburnt or **dehydrated** as this could lead to:

- Headaches and migraines
- Dizzy spells
- Sunburn
- Premature (early) aging
- Skin cancer.

The winter months also come with challenges for outdoor workers; some days are cold, windy and rainy, so workers are more likely to catch illnesses such as coughs and colds. Outdoor workers may have to work in areas where the air is not a clean as it should be. Examples are heavy traffic, exposure to fertilisers used on farms and chemicals from factories. This could lead to illnesses such as:

- Chest infections
- Lung cancer
- **Frostbite**
- Skin irritations
- Allergies.

Concentration span

Some job roles can be very demanding and you need to be patient. You might have to concentrate for long periods of time and remain focused on what you are doing. You can improve your concentration span by doing the following things:

- Concentrate on one task at a time
- Avoid getting distracted
- Have regular rest breaks
- Drink plenty of fluids.

Postmen have to cope with all weather conditions. Can you think of other outdoor jobs?

✱ Key terms

Dehydrated
Not having enough water in the body.

Frostbite
Where body tissues, especially on the fingers, toes and nose are permanently damaged by severe cold.

Shift work

Some jobs involve working unusual hours and these hours can be spread over several days of the week. You might have to work weekends, nights and public holidays. This is referred to as **shift work**. Shift work can be both physically and mentally demanding on a person's wellbeing, so shift workers need to be in good health to cope.

High adrenaline jobs

Some jobs have to be completed very fast and people who work in these types of jobs need to be able to think and react very quickly. High adrenaline jobs can be very stressful and you would have to work under a lot of pressure.

Activity: How do I protect myself?

1. What products should workers use to protect themselves when working outdoors in the summer?
2. Why should outdoor workers use these products?
3. What types of clothing could they wear to protect them from the sun?
4. Why should they wear the clothing you have identified?
5. What might happen if they did not use the things you have suggested?

Check

- Many job roles have health requirements linked to them
- A person's job depends on their own health
- It is your responsibility to ensure that you are healthy enough for your job role.

* **Key term**

Shift work
Working different times on a regular basis. For example 9am to 5pm, 5pm to 1am, 1am to 9am.

29

L02 Health risks: physical & verbal abuse

All work settings are different and each place of work will come with its own health risks and hazards that you will need to be aware of and avoid to stay well and healthy at work.

Physical and verbal abuse

Most roles in health and social care focus on caring for others. This means that you will be dealing with the general public on a regular basis and will have a lot of contact with the following:

- Service users
- Service users' families
- Service users' friends
- Contractors (e.g. maintenance staff)
- Other members of staff.

This can sometimes cause problems and there are occasions when staff are verbally and physically abused by the people that they are looking after or their relatives. This can be because some of the people that you are caring for may have medical conditions that cause them to behave aggressively towards others.

Relatives may also become abusive because they are upset and concerned about their loved one.

In your job, you will need to find ways to avoid situations where you could experience **verbal abuse** or **physical abuse**, and learn how to deal with such situations, which will be helpful to your own health and wellbeing.

Most health care establishments employ security staff to help with awkward situations, and some supply their staff with personal alarms and offer training for staff on how to deal with abusive clients.

It is useful to know how to communicate in a calm manner as this will help to control the situation and may ensure that it does not get worse.

Bullying

Bullying comes in many forms:

- Harassing – to continually bother or annoy another person
- Mistreating – to treat someone badly

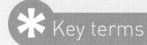

Key terms

Verbal abuse
When someone is shouted at or spoken to rudely or insultingly.

Physical abuse
When someone is hit or attacked.

Bullying
Treating someone badly.

Why might a nurse be subject to abuse?

- Ignoring – not paying attention to someone

- Discriminating – treating someone unfairly because of their race, religion, gender, sexuality or ability

- Hitting or smacking – to strike a person with your hand or an object.

Case study:
Play nicely

Sophie and Charlotte are making sandcastles in the sandpit and Abby wants to join in. Sophie and Charlotte take no notice of Abby and they throw sand at her and tell her to go away.

1. Are Sophie and Charlotte bullying Abby?

2. If this is bullying, what form of bullying is it?

3. What could you do, to help the three girls get along?

Check

- There are many health risks in care settings
- You may be verbally or physically abused
- It is important that you know how to keep yourself safe.

L02 Health risks: special equipment

There are various pieces of specialist equipment available for workers to use in their job roles. This equipment comes in many forms and it is provided to help employees perform their roles in a safe and healthy way. Specialist equipment includes:

- Steps/ladder – a piece of movable equipment used to reach objects in high places

- Knee pads – pieces of soft material used to protect your knees when you are kneeling

- Hoist – a piece of equipment used to raise or lift someone

- Pat slide – a patient sliding board used to transfer a patient from one bed to another

- Wheelchair – a chair with wheels used by people who are unable to walk

- Trolley – a bed on wheels used to transport patients from one area to another.

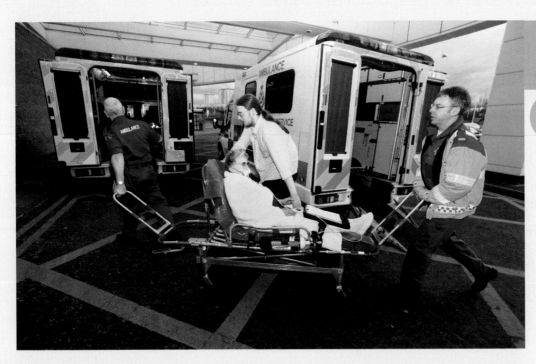

How does this equipment protect the health of the ambulance staff?

Transporting chemicals

There will be many times when you will need to use chemicals within your job role. Chemicals come in many different forms and you must make sure that you work with them safely, check guidelines and ask if you are unsure. Chemicals widely used in care settings are medicines and cleaning products.

! Remember

When appropriate:

- Wear goggles
- Wear a face mask
- Wear gloves
- Keep lids on bottles
- Carry only light weights
- Use lifting equipment, e.g. trolleys, to move people around
- Put equipment safely away when not being used.

Manual handling

This is the term used to describe any form of moving or lifting, and all employers must offer their staff training in manual handling. Incorrect manual handling can result in accidents and injuries and can cause many lost working hours. Therefore, it is important that safe manual handling procedures are adhered to by all members of staff. Before moving you should ask yourself:

- Does the person or object have to be moved?
- Can what needs to be done be completed where the object or person already is?

Back injury

It is widely recognised that people who work in health and social care settings are more likely to suffer from back pain and injuries. This is due to the nature of some of the tasks involved within care work, particularly the moving, lifting, pushing and pulling that is involved. It is important that you protect yourself from such injuries, and you use equipment that is specifically designed for lifting and moving clients and objects.

Case study:

Assistance going to the toilet

Wendy has recently had an operation. She is unable to get out of bed and move about on her own. She has called you and said she needs to go to the toilet.

1. What equipment could you use to help her get out of bed?

2. What could you use to transport her to the toilet?

✓ Check

- There is a variety of specialist equipment to ensure your safety at work
- Chemicals need to be transported and used with care
- Following the correct manual handling procedures will help prevent back injuries.

L02 Health risks: minor injuries, infection & stress

Many injuries at work are caused by very small slips, falls or trips. These accidents can be caused by:

- Icy surfaces
- Badly fitted carpets
- Wet or damp floors
- Shiny or greasy floors
- Damaged or loose flooring
- Objects and clutter in the way
- Uneven flooring
- Wearing incorrect footwear.

Injuries caused by slips, falls or trips include:

- Bruises
- Broken bones
- Sprains
- Cuts
- Back injuries
- Head injuries.

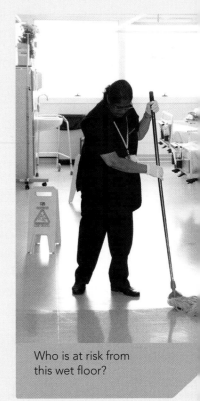

Who is at risk from this wet floor?

Spread of infection

You will come across infections many times within health and social care settings and it is your duty to ensure that you help to reduce the spread of them. Infections are caused by **viruses**, **bacteria** and **micro-organisms** that can be found in the environment, humans and animals and these can be spread in four main ways.

Inhalation

Some infections are carried in the air that you breathe and are spread by droplets produced by coughing and sneezing.

Direct contact

Someone or something with an infection contaminates another object, person or animal by directly touching it.

Ingestion

Many infections are caught when bacteria grow on the food and drink that we eat.

Body fluids

Some infections can be carried in body fluids, such as blood, semen and saliva. These infections are usually spread by injection with a syringe, through cuts in the skin, or sexual contact, for example HIV and hepatitis.

✱ Key terms

Virus
A tiny infectious particle that can cause disease.

Bacteria
Micro-organisms that can cause disease.

Micro-organism
Very small microscopic living thing. Some micro-organisms cause disease.

As a care worker it is vital that you do everything within your power to ensure you reduce the spread of infection. This will not only safeguard your own health, but it will also help reduce the spread of infection to your patients.

Stress

Stress is an emotion that some people feel when too much pressure is put on them and this can be a problem in the workplace. A small amount of stress can sometimes be a good thing as it can make workers more productive. However, if a person's work load is very demanding, it can result in them feeling completely overwhelmed and they can then become stressed and ill. Stress affects people in many different ways and symptoms can vary from person to person. They can include:

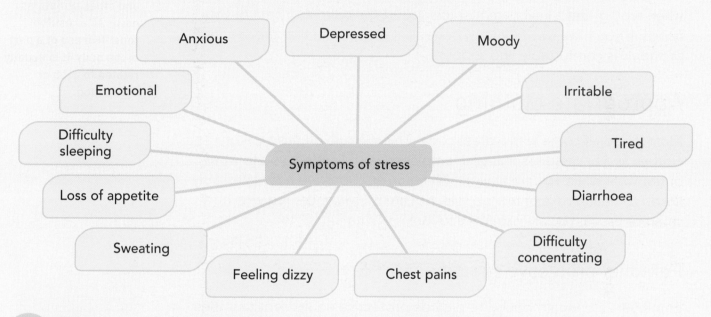

Activity: Stressful work

1. Make a list of jobs that you think are *not* stressful.
2. Make a list of jobs that you think *could* be stressful.
3. Which jobs do you think would be *the most* stressful?
4. Why do you think some jobs are more stressful than others?

Check

- Slips, falls or trips can cause many injuries at work
- Infections can be spread easily
- Stress affects people in different ways and can lead to illness.

L02 Reducing health risks

At work it is important that both you and your employer do as much as possible to reduce risks to your health that may be connected with your job role.

Appropriate equipment

All equipment supplied for your job role should be in good working order and you should only use equipment that is suitable for the task it has been designed for. For example, to reduce the risk of **repetitive strain injury** when typing, use a keyboard rest to support the palm and heel of your hands. If you have to sit for long periods, it is essential that the seating provided is comfortable and supportive.

Appropriate clothing

Most job roles come with a dress code. This is a rule on the type of clothes and accessories that your employer would expect you to wear or not wear while you are at work. Some dress codes are not necessarily linked to health risks of the job role, but are more concerned with how smart or casual you are expected to look.

Personal protective equipment (PPE)

Employers are legally bound to provide protective equipment that their employees need to perform their job role safely.

Here are some examples of personal protective equipment.

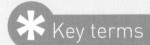
Key terms

Repetitive strain injury (RSI)
A condition where pain and other symptoms occur as a result of repetitive use of a part of the body. It is usually related to a job or occupation.

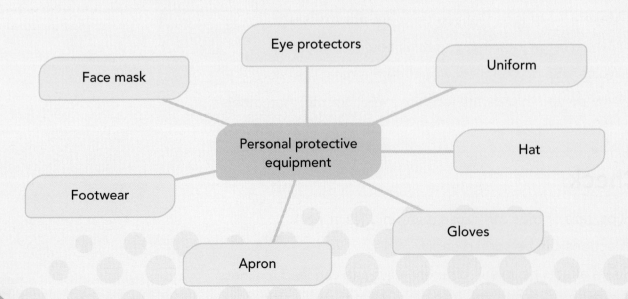

Training and knowledge of procedures and rules

It is up to your employer to make sure that you are trained and aware of their procedures and rules. However, it is up to you to ensure you have understood them.

Food safety rules

Food safety rules reduce the possibility of people becoming sick from eating food that has been contaminated by bacteria. They ensure that food has been prepared in a clean, suitable environment and that all food is safe and healthy to eat.

Vaccination of staff

Vaccines are substances that are put directly into the body (usually by injection) to produce immunity to a disease. Health and social care workers are offered vaccinations because the people that they may be caring for are more vulnerable to infections.

Activity: Health risks

Choose three different areas of work and produce a leaflet that describes potential health risks to:

- Staff

- Service users

- Others.

Check

- Rules and equipment are in place to maintain good health at work

- Food must be prepared in a safe manner

- Vaccinations protect you and your patients.

Remember

- Wash your hands with soap and hot water prior to touching food

- Clean and wash down all surfaces

- Clean the utensils you are using

- Use different chopping boards/ utensils for raw and cooked meats and poultry

- Prepare salads and vegetables separately from raw meats and poultry

- Use food within its use by date

- Serve food at a safe temperature.

Functional skills

By producing a leaflet, you will be demonstrating your English writing skills.

ASSESSMENT OVERVIEW

While working through this unit, you will have prepared for completing the following assessment tasks:

○	1.1 Explain different health requirements for a chosen area of work	Pages 20–29
○	2.1 Describe health risks for a chosen area of work	Pages 30–35
○	2.2 Explain how to reduce health risks in a chosen area of work	Pages 36–37

Assignment tips

- To help you pass this unit, you should clearly identify a specific area of work and make a poster that explains three different health requirements for your chosen area.

- Give information on each health requirement with examples to support what you have said.

- Produce a leaflet that describes at least three health risks found within your chosen area of work.

- Your leaflet must include information on how to reduce the health risks you have described.

HEALTH & SOCIAL CARE NEEDS

When you are working in a health or social care environment, it is useful to find out about the needs of the service users that you will be working with. Everyone is different and has particular needs. Learning about their specific needs, will enable you to help service users with any tasks or activities that they carry out.

This unit helps you to learn and gain an understanding of the range of physical, emotional and social needs that a service user may have. It also explores what health and social care is available for individuals.

In this unit you will:

- Learn about our health needs and how our health is affected by different things

- Look at what health needs individuals have

- Investigate what health care and social care is available for individuals

How do people's needs vary?

L01 Physical health needs

People have basic human **needs** which must be met in order to survive. These are often described as physical needs, emotional needs and social needs.

Food and water

No one can survive without food and water for a long period of time. The average human can live without food for up to approximately 30 to 40 days, but can survive without water for only three to four days.

Warmth, shelter, fresh air and a safe environment

As a human, you have a physical need to feel safe. A place where you feel safe is often at home as it provides you with shelter from the outside world. Most people will also feel safe in a health and social care setting that is warm, clean and organised. It is also important for your health to get regular fresh air.

Hygiene

Good hygiene is an important physical need because if you have poor hygiene you can become very ill. You must make sure that you follow basic hygiene rules such as washing your hands after visiting the toilet. Poor personal hygiene can give a bad impression, making it difficult to make and keep friends.

Medical care

At some point in your life, you will probably need to receive some form of medical care. The treatment could vary from visiting your local shop to buy cold medicine, to visiting your **GP** or receiving treatment in a hospital. Without access to medical care when you need it you could become very ill.

Changing health needs

As you get older your needs change. Think about the differing health needs of babies, children, adults and older people.

✳ Key terms

Need
Something that is necessary to live a healthy life.

GP
General practitioner or family doctor.

Some medical care is available to buy in local shops

Here are some very important physical needs:

- Eat sufficient food

- Drink plenty of water

- Wear clothing

- Have at least eight hours sleep a night.

Activity: Physical needs

Make a poster to put on the wall of your classroom or your bedroom that describes your physical needs.

Functional skills

By making a poster, you will be demonstrating your **English** writing skills.

Check

- Everyone has physical needs that have to be met in order to live

- Some needs remain the same, but some needs change as you get older

- Not meeting your physical needs can mean that you become ill or die.

L01 Emotional & social health needs

Love/emotional support

Feeling loved and cared about can really help to support people through difficult times in their lives. Love and emotional support doesn't have to come from someone you are in a relationship with – it can just be having someone that will listen to you, for example a friend or counsellor.

Independence

As a child you have little **independence**. As you get older you may ask to do certain things by yourself, such as walking to the shops on your own or with your friends. Independence is good because it gives you a sense of freedom.

Stimulation

Have you ever returned to school after a long break (such as the school holiday) and forgotten how to access your email? You know that regular physical exercise helps keep the body healthy. In the same way, mental exercise can help keep the brain healthy and working. It needs **stimulation**.

Self-esteem

This is how much you value yourself and your life. Having a high self-esteem may make you feel happy and confident, whereas a low self-esteem may lead to depression and unhappiness.

Social interaction

This is an important need because by interacting with other people you learn to develop as a human being. You learn from an early age to walk and talk, and as you get older you understand how to behave in particular situations and learn manners.

Social interaction is also good because if you are upset or worried about something, friends and family can be there to talk things through and to support you. Support can be found in other places but will often involve some kind of social interaction, for example going to see a counsellor or ringing a helpline.

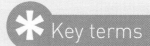
Key terms

Independence
Making your own decisions and not needing other people's help.

Stimulation
Encouraging something to develop.

Social interaction
Having contact with other people.

It is important for children to interact socially with one another from a young age

Activity: Your physical, emotional and social needs

What needs do you require to live happily and comfortably every day? Think about your daily routine from when you get up to going to bed.

Make a list of all your needs. Remember to say whether they are physical, emotional or social.

Check

- Emotional and social health needs are different from physical health needs

- Emotional and social health needs make us feel supported and loved

- Not meeting our emotional and social health needs can affect our independence and self-esteem.

L02 How health is affected by different factors

Lots of different things can make us ill or feel rundown, or affect our health more seriously, for example by causing cancer.

Illness and disability

Having a medical condition or a disability can cause additional health problems because they may prevent you from keeping active and fit. They may also prevent you from going out and socialising with your friends or going to work, which could have an effect on your mental health.

Housing

Not everyone lives in good housing. Some people live in houses or flats that are damp and rundown. Living in bad conditions can make health problems, such as asthma much worse.

Some areas of the country have a bad reputation which can make the people that live there stressed because they feel unsafe.

Pollution

Air pollution comes from car fumes, factories, cigarette smoke and many other places. This pollution can have a negative effect on our health by making some conditions, such as **emphysema** worse. It can also cause symptoms such as headaches, nausea, and allergic reactions and contribute towards long-term health problems like lung cancer.

> **✱ Key term**
>
> **Emphysema**
> A disease in the lungs making it hard to breathe.

Where you live can affect your health.

Poverty and unemployment

Being **unemployed** can lead to being in **poverty**. Having little or no income can affect you in many ways. You may become depressed about having no money as you may not be able to afford to go out with friends or buy new clothes or expensive foods.

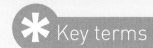

Activity: What factors can affect your health?

A health care centre asks you to make a leaflet that informs people of the different factors that can affect their health. Make your leaflet as informative and detailed as possible.

Hint: Think of yourself, friends, family or other people you know. What factors make them healthy or unhealthy?

Functional skills

By making a leaflet, you will be demonstrating your English writing skills.

Check

- There are lots of factors that can affect your health positively and negatively

- Having little or no money can affect you physically, emotionally and socially

- One in two people with disabilities is unemployed.

Lifestyle factors affecting our health

Your lifestyle choices can have an impact on both your physical and mental health.

Smoking

It is well known that smoking is bad for your health as it can cause lung cancer and **chronic respiratory disease** as well as many other illnesses. By law, packets of cigarettes have to give big, visible warnings about the dangers of smoking, and some packets even have pictures of the damage that cigarettes can do to your body.

Drug and alcohol misuse

Drug and alcohol misuse has been linked to depression and mental health illnesses, such as **schizophrenia**, as well as causing damage to your body.

When you think of drugs, you tend to think of illegal ones, such as heroin, cocaine and cannabis. You tend to forget about drugs that doctors give you. Some people can become addicted to the tablets their GP prescribes them.

Obesity and exercise

Doctors in Britain are worried that people are getting fat and not exercising enough. There are lots of news items and television programmes about obesity such as *Fat Camp* and *You Are What You Eat*. It can be very convenient to buy food that is bad for you, such as chicken nuggets and chips, as junk food can be quite cheap and easy to make. Although this food fits into our busy lifestyle, it should only be eaten occasionally.

As well as eating correctly, you must exercise as being overweight can dangerously affect how long you live for. Doctors recommend that you exercise regularly and suggest that a brisk walk for 30 minutes five days a week is a good start.

You need to avoid eating too much junk food to keep healthy

✳ Key terms

Chronic respiratory disease
A long-lasting disease of the lungs.

Schizophrenia
A mental illness that can affect your behaviour, thinking and emotions.

To stay healthy, remember the following:

- Do 30 minutes of exercise, five days a week

- Eat five portions of fruit and vegetables every day

- Don't smoke

- Drink lots of water

- Only have one or two small glasses of alcohol a day, or less

- Don't binge drink.

Case study:
Moreum's health

Moreum is a 25-year-old woman who has severe asthma. She lives in the middle of a very busy city and struggles to get about because her asthma leaves her breathless. Moreum finds it very hard to exercise due to her asthma, and is overweight.

Moreum does not have a job, but looks forward to going out in the evenings with her friends to the local pub for a few alcoholic drinks and a kebab on the way home. Moreum also smokes when she is with her friends and has tried a few recreational drugs.

1. What factors do you think are affecting Moreum's health?

2. In what ways are they affecting her?

3. What advice would you give to Moreum to help her improve her health?

Check

- Your choice of lifestyle can affect how healthy you are

- Smoking can cause respiratory illnesses and cancer

- Drug and alcohol misuse can cause physical and mental health problems

- A bad diet can make you overweight and influence how long you live.

L03 Health needs of children & teenagers

People's basic needs vary depending on their age or their health. Earlier in this unit, you learnt that our health needs can be separated into different categories: physical, emotional and social.

Babies and young children

Babies and young children have a lot of similar needs. They both require the same physical needs. For example, lots of sleep, food, water and to be kept warm and safe.

Babies and young children both need a routine for eating and sleeping. This routine will develop as they get older to allow for social needs, such as playing with toys and other children and interacting with people. Babies and young children need to explore their surroundings as this is how they learn about the world around them.

Emotionally, babies and young children differ. Both need a lot of love and to bond with their carers, but young children also require some independence, which helps to improve their self-esteem.

These are important things to remember when looking after babies and small children:

- Keep them warm. Babies cannot control their own temperature

- Stick to a routine for eating and sleeping

- Keep them clean

- Provide toys that are bright, colourful and have different textures.

Adolescents

Adolescence is one of the most difficult stages of life. It is when you usually go through puberty and start to change into an adult. Changes in hormone levels mean that emotions can become confused and you may feel under a lot of stress. You also have exams to take at school and start asking for more independence at home.

Key term

Adolescence
The stage in a young person's life when they become sexually mature.

Here are the health needs of an adolescent:

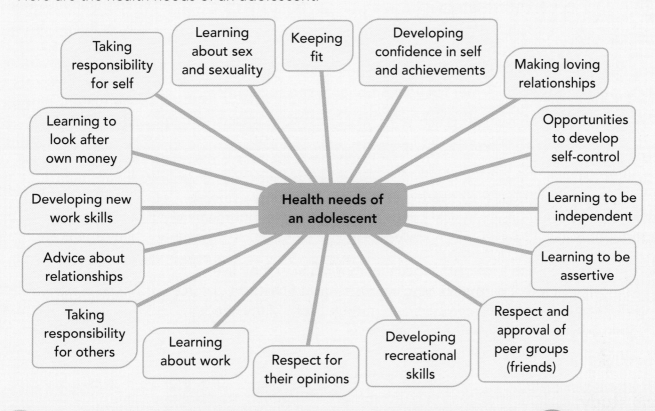

Activity: Desert island

Imagine that you are stranded on a desert island. On a large piece of paper, draw your island. Until you are rescued, what are your needs? What do you need to do in order to survive? Make a list.

Check your list. Are these things that you actually need or things that you want?

Present your island and needs to the class.

Functional skills

By presenting your island and needs to the class, you will be demonstrating your English speaking skills.

Check

- Babies and young children have similar needs
- Babies and young children need lots of attention, stimulation and play
- Adolescents experience puberty and need more independence.

L03 Health needs of adults

As you get older your needs develop and change. Generally, your physical needs remain the same, but your emotional and social needs alter as you age.

Adults

The health needs of adults are as varied as they are for younger people. Adults have the same basic physical needs as young people, but their emotional and social needs are very varied.

Adults have to deal with a lot of changes that may occur in their lives, such as moving in with a partner, buying a house, having children, divorce, losing close friends or family members and getting a job. Many needs develop in adults as a result of these changes.

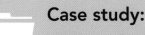

Case study:

What's wrong with Michael?

Michael is 54 years old. He used to be a train driver, which paid well. Recently, Michael lost his job due to being drunk at work on more than one occasion, and is now unemployed.

Since losing his job, Michael has not been able to keep up with the mortgage payments on his house that he lived in with his wife and children. The house has been repossessed by the bank and Michael has moved into a two bedroom flat on a social housing estate. The flat is cold and damp. Michael's wife has left him and taken the children with her. Michael isn't eating properly as he has never had to cook for himself and is losing a lot of weight. He feels very lonely and unloved and Michael's doctor is concerned about his health.

1. What factors do you think are affecting Michael's health?

2. In what ways are they affecting him?

Older people

The changes that occur for many older adults as they retire are life changing. However, for many **retirement** is an experience to look forward to, with time to travel or do other things that they have not had time to do while at work.

Sadly, this is not always the case. Some adults are not able to be as active in their retirement as others because they are not as healthy as they used to be. They may also lose a partner and friends through old age and many people fall into poverty on retirement.

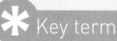

Key term

Retirement
Giving up work.

Getting older can be quite lonely for some individuals

Check

- Our needs develop and change over time
- Adults and older people have the same basic physical needs as young children and babies
- Adults have more emotional and social needs
- Older people may need more help with their basic physical needs
- Older people may not be as healthy as they used to be.

L03 Health needs of a particular group

People with disabilities have special needs. Disabilities can be inherited and present from birth or acquired as a result of an accident or an illness. These conditions can affect health and people with disabilities may often have specific health needs. Needs will vary depending on each individual's circumstances.

Physical disabilities

A physical disability is a condition that affects an individual's mobility/movement or one or more of the senses (sight, hearing, smell, taste and touch). When people think of disabilities, they tend to think of someone who cannot walk and uses a wheelchair but there are lots of different physical disabilities and you must be aware of their individual needs.

Learning disabilities

Some people have a **learning disability** which means the learning ability and/or development of the brain are impaired. It can affect skills including the ability to speak, listen, read, write, spell, reason and organise information.

Mental illness

A **mental illness** is a health condition that affects an individual's thinking, emotions or behaviour. A mental illness can make it hard for the individual to handle everyday situations and feelings.

Acute and chronic illnesses

An acute illness arrives quickly and **usually only lasts for a short period of time, for example a cold or flu.** A chronic illness is an illness that can be with someone all their life, for example asthma, or it can be an illness that lasts a long time, or reoccurs. People with illnesses have specific health needs.

Cerrie Burnell is a successful children's television presenter despite her physical disability.

✳ Key terms

Learning disability
A condition that prevents someone from learning basic skills or information at the same rate or to the same level as most people of the same age.

Mental illness
A health condition that changes a person's thinking feelings, or behaviour.

Terminal illness

A **terminal illness** eventually causes the death of a patient. The illness can last a long time, but the individual often becomes less able and independent as the illness progresses.

 Key term

Terminal illness
An illness that will lead to the death of the patient.

 ## Activity: Who needs what?

Make a table that describes the physical, emotional and social needs of **the different groups covered in this unit**. Remember that some needs may be the same between particular groups, but others may be different.

Physical needs	Emotional needs	Social needs

 ## Check

- There are lots of different types of disability and each has its own needs

- Disabilities may have physical needs, emotional needs and/or social needs

- It is important to know the specific needs of the user of the service

L04 Available health care for individuals

You are lucky to live in a society that gives us free health care when we need it. This is called the National Health Service (**NHS**). The NHS provides health care from hospitals, dentists, family doctors and many more to keep us all fit and well.

General practitioner

A general practitioner (GP) is another name for your family doctor. Your GP is often the first person you will go and see if you are unwell. They will give you a check up and may give you some advice on how to stay healthy or a **prescription** for some medicine to help you get better, or they can refer you on to a specialist who knows more about your condition.

Dentist

A dentist specialises in keeping our teeth healthy. They give us advice on how to look after our teeth and gums.

You would usually visit your dentist in a local surgery where they give you a check-up and perform any necessary work on your teeth, such as fillings. Sometimes they refer you to a dentist at a hospital who carries out more specialist work.

Pharmacy

A **pharmacy** sells lots of basic medicines without you having to visit your GP. Dispensing pharmacies take your prescription and give you the right amount of medicine that the doctor has requested. They can give you advice on how to take the medicine.

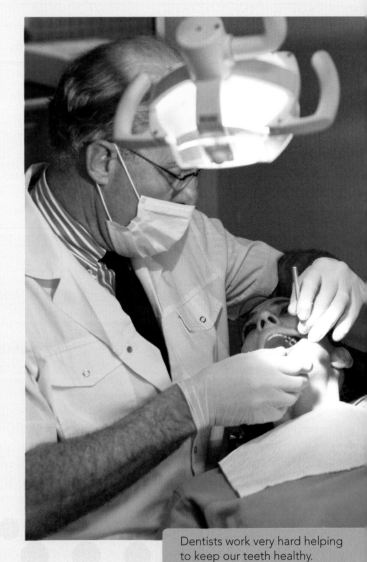

✳ Key terms

Prescription
A written note from a doctor telling a chemist what medicine to give out.

Pharmacy
Another name for a chemist shop.

Dentists work very hard helping to keep our teeth healthy.

Case study:

Where should Madeleine go?

Madeleine's mouth is very sore. Every time she eats or drinks something very hot or very cold, she feels a lot of pain at the front of her mouth.

Madeleine tells her mother who buys her some painkillers from the pharmacy. Madeleine's best friend, Syeda, says that Madeleine should go and see her GP. Madeleine's Aunty Robyn thinks that Madeleine should go to her dentist.

1. **Where do you think Madeleine should go? Why?**

2. **How would a pharmacy help Madeleine?**

3. **How would a GP help Madeleine?**

4. **How would a dentist help Madeleine?**

Check

- NHS stands for the National Health Service

- The NHS provides free health care

- A pharmacy can give you health advice and sells medication.

L04 Additional health care for individuals

Sometimes more care is needed than just a visit to your local GP, dentist or pharmacy. You may need extra help to get better or to gain your independence.

Hospital inpatient and outpatient

Hospitals have two types of patient:

- *Inpatient*: a patient who needs to stay in hospital for at least one night to have particular medical treatment. Patients who have operations or treatment that may make them very ill often stay in hospital for one or more nights so that their condition can be monitored.

- *Outpatient*: a patient who has treatment at a hospital but does not need to stay the night. This could be for a blood test, X-ray or **biopsy**, for example.

Physiotherapy

Physiotherapy is carried out on individuals who have particular problems with movement, for instance following an injury. Physiotherapists monitor the patient and give them special exercises to improve their **mobility** or relieve any pain that the movement may cause.

Occupational therapy

Occupational therapy helps individuals to carry out everyday activities, such as bathing, brushing their teeth, getting dressed or eating. This is an important job as some people may not be able to carry out these tasks particularly well as a result of an accident, disability, illness or an operation.

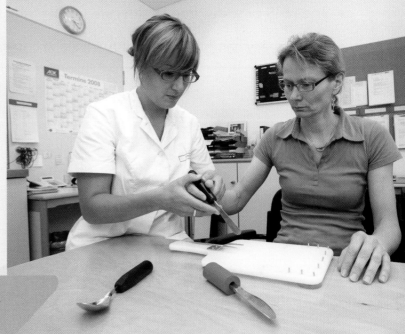

An occupational therapist helping a patient with a daily task.

Home nursing

Home nursing is available for individual clients or couples. A nurse visits the patient in their home as often as required depending on their needs. It is particularly useful for patients who may have just returned home from having surgery, or it can provide **respite** when a regular nurse, carer or family member needs a break.

Case study:

Anais

Anais is 84 and has very bad arthritis in her hands and sores on her legs. She cannot get around much by herself. Once a day she is visited by a home nurse who treats her sores and gives her a weekly vitamin injection.

Anais has recently had an operation on her hands, which required her to spend a week in hospital. The occupational therapist gave Anais a long-handled hairbrush, toothbrush and knife and fork to help her with her normal daily routine while she recovers.

Once a week Anais sees the physiotherapist who gives her hand exercises to keep the joints mobile. Anais visits the hospital once a month to see her doctor to check on her progress.

From this case study, you can see that Anais receives a variety of services.

1. What services is Anais receiving?

2. How are they helping her?

3. Does she need any other services?

✓ Check

- There are lots of different services that can help you to get better
- All the services work together as a team to help you
- You can get help in your own home if you need it.

✳ Key term

Respite
When an unpaid carer takes a break while their caring duties are covered by a paid worker.

L04 Available social care for individuals

Social care provides users of the service with practical help and support. Social care can range from receiving help around your house, to attending a day centre twice a week for company and activities.

Community care

Community care is mainly for elderly people, people with learning or physical disabilities or a mental illness, and is provided outside a hospital setting and in the community. The aim is to help you carry on living in your home with as much independence as possible.

Home care

Home care-workers help look after people in their own homes. They generally provide personal care, such as help with washing and dressing, preparing meals and other activities of daily life. They visit as often as the user of the service needs.

Day care

Day care is often provided to individuals who are suffering from **dementia**. Users of the service are picked up from their home and taken to the day care centre where they can participate in a number of activities aimed at stimulating the brain. The care provided can also involve practical help, such as **chiropody**.

Some people may need assistance for basic tasks, such as eating

Older people enjoying themselves at a day care centre

* Key terms

Dementia
When the brain starts to deteriorate and functions such as memory start to weaken.

Chiropody
Care and treatment of the feet.

Children's and adult's residential care

Residential care is provided for children and adults who cannot live in their own homes for various reasons. Children tend to move into a home for a period of time while their living conditions are improved, whereas adults move into a residential home and are looked after by trained staff if they cannot cope with day-to-day tasks independently.

Respite care

Respite care is different from other types of care as it is aimed at those doing the caring, that is those who give unpaid help to their friends or family members. Respite care allows the carer to take a short break while a professional takes over the caring duties.

Activity: What care is in your area?

In groups, identify and describe the kinds of places of care that you have seen in your local area. You might have passed one on your way home. You may even have a relative in one, or perhaps you have seen advertisements on the back of the local bus.

Check

- Health and social care isn't just about people going to their GP or hospital

- Social care services are there to help individuals live as independent and active a life as possible

- There are social care services that give carers a break.

ASSESSMENT OVERVIEW

While working through this unit, you will have prepared for completing the following assessment tasks:

○	1.1	Identify and describe the significance of physical health needs	Pages 40–41
○	1.2	Identify and describe the significance of emotional and social health needs	Page 42–43
○	2.1	Describe different factors that affect health	Pages 44–47
○	3.1	Describe the health needs of individuals	Pages 48–53
○	4.1	Outline health care available for individuals	Pages 54–57
○	4.2	Outline social care available for individuals	Pages 58–59

Assignment tips

- To help you pass this unit, produce a poster with titles and pictures of a number of physical, emotional and social needs.

- Make sure you include definitions of the different needs.

- You could look at different case studies of people, or carry out interviews, to find out what factors can affect how healthy you are.

- To show your understanding of the health and social care that is available, use the case studies as a starting point to make information leaflets, telling individuals where they can go to receive health and social care services to meet their needs.

PERSONAL CARE IN HEALTH & SOCIAL CARE

Personal care involves looking after your body. You will need help and support with your personal care at some point during your life. Think back to when you were a baby or a child and the types of things that you needed help with. As you have got older, you have most likely become more independent and need less or no help with most personal care tasks.

However, some people are never able to fully take care of themselves or events may happen in people's lives that mean they become dependent on others for their personal care needs.

This unit introduces you to the types of people that have personal care needs and helps you to discover the skills and personal qualities needed for the personal care of others. It also helps you to understand why it is important to follow procedures when giving personal care.

In this unit you will:

- Learn about the personal care needs of individuals

- Explore the skills and personal qualities needed for the personal care of others

- Understand why it is important to follow the health and social care setting's procedures when providing personal care

Babies need help with their personal care. Can you think of other people that may need assistance?

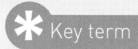

L01 Personal care needs

People have various different care needs.

Washing

It is really important that your body is kept clean and **hygienic**. Keeping clean makes you feel and look good. Good personal hygiene can also stop germs from getting into your body or spreading to others.

Some people find it difficult to bath or shower themselves and have to get others to help them. Being unable to wash yourself is not very nice for you or others around you. Here are some of the effects of poor personal hygiene:

- Unclean and greasy hair
- Body odour
- Dirty nails
- Bacteria feed off dead skin cells.

Dressing

Wearing clean and suitable clothing is important to your personal care needs. Underwear has contact with the most personal parts of your body and should be washed and changed every day. Washing clothes regularly will help to reduce the amount of bacteria on them, reduce the amount of infections you may get and prevent you from smelling unpleasant.

Feeding

You must have food and water to live. Being able to feed yourself with the right amount of food and water is essential to maintain good health. Feeding ourselves is one of the first skills that we learn from a very young age. However, there are several groups of people that may need help with this:

- Users of wheelchairs
- People with learning difficulties
- People that are visually impaired

- Babies and young children
- Sick people
- Older people.

> **Key term**
>
> **Hygienic**
> **Free from dirt and germs.**

Why is it important for babies to be changed frequently?

If these people do not have help with eating and drinking, their health could suffer and they could become very sick or ill.

Going to the toilet

Being able to use the toilet when we need to is very important to our wellbeing. Some groups of people are unable to take themselves to the toilet and they might:

- Have wet or soiled themselves
- Get infections
- Smell unpleasant.

✳ Key term

Commode
A movable toilet.

Case study:

I can't do it for myself

Julie has just had an emergency operation to remove her gall bladder and has been told she is not to get out of bed for at least twenty-four hours. Julie wants to go to the toilet and has asked the nurse on several occasions for a **commode**. The nurse, however, appears busy and has not brought the commode to Julie who is getting increasingly upset.

1. How do you think Julie might be feeling?

2. Why is Julie upset?

3. What could happen to Julie if the nurse does not bring her a commode?

✓ Check

- Personal care is important for your health and wellbeing
- Everyone is entitled to have their personal care needs met
- Some people need help with their personal care needs.

L01 The emotional needs of individuals

Being happy is important to your health and wellbeing, so it is important when caring for others that you consider their emotional needs.

Respect

Everyone has the right to be listened to and treated in a way that considers their feelings. This is called respect and everyone also has the right to be respected. If you respect someone, it can have a big effect on how they feel.

Privacy

Everyone has a right to privacy and all personal hygiene tasks should be performed in private, with doors closed or curtains pulled round. You should discuss a service users' personal information in private and where others cannot hear what is being said. Furthermore, service users should be able to make personal phone calls in private and all information held on them must be stored safely and only disclosed to others on a 'need to know' basis.

Dignity

Treating a person in a dignified way shows that you respect and value them. It also shows you are thinking about them as an individual and are concerned about their feelings and pride. Treating a person with **dignity** boosts their self-esteem and helps them to trust you.

✳ Key term

Dignity
Feeling of pride or value.

Choice

Giving people choice allows them to be in control of their own care and makes them feel that they are being listened to. Think about how you would feel if someone else told you what to do each day and you were not allowed to make any decisions for yourself.

Independence

Independence is about being able to do things for yourself and it is important that people become and remain independent as much as possible throughout their lives. Being independent begins from a very early age when you start to learn simple skills that you can do on your own. As you get older, these skills will develop and you will be able to do more difficult things for yourself. Eventually, you should be able to do almost everything on your own and will not have to rely on anyone to help you with your personal care needs.

Case study:

What can I watch?

Emily is 92 years old and has recently moved into Rooks Residential Care Home. There is a lounge where all of the residents watch television. The manager of the home has told Emily that the other residents don't like watching the same programmes as Emily and she is now unable to watch her favourite programmes.

1. How would you feel if you were Emily?

2. What should the manager do?

3. What might happen if Emily is not allowed to watch programmes of her own choice?

Check

- Everyone has emotional needs
- People are happier when doing things for themselves
- Respecting people and giving them choices is important to their health and wellbeing.

L01 Individuals with personal care needs

Everyone has personal care needs and these differ according to various factors such as:

- Age
- Ability
- Disability
- Culture.

However, it is important that you treat each person as an individual and consider their care needs on a personal basis.

Babies and young children

Babies are dependent on their main carers from the day they are born and someone must feed, wash and take responsibility for all their personal care needs for them to survive. Babies are born with **reflexes** that help them to survive. These reflexes are:

- Crying
- Sucking
- Grasping.

As babies get older they develop into young children and begin to build skills that enable them to do more things for themselves. Most young children develop very quickly and as their skills increase, they want to make their own choices and become more independent. However, they still depend on their main carers to provide a safe and loving environment and to supervise and guide them.

Adults

Adulthood starts around the age of eighteen. By the time you become an adult, you will more than likely be able to care for all of your own personal care needs; being able to wash, dress, feed and care for yourself. Most adults are fully independent and make decisions for themselves. However, an accident or illness can change this.

 Key term

Reflex
Something that happens automatically without thinking.

Case study:

Care after an accident

Laura is 28 years old and works full-time as a supervisor in a local supermarket. On her way to work she was involved in a car accident, which has left her with a broken arm and leg. She is now in hospital and is unable to get out of bed.

1. **What things do you think Laura can do for herself?**

2. **What personal care will others have to help Laura with?**

3. **Explain how carers can help maintain Laura's dignity and privacy?**

4. **How do you think Laura feels?**

5. **What can Laura do about the situation?**

Elderly frail adults

As you get older and reach the elderly stage of your life, lots of changes happen. Older people retire from work and most look forward to the freedom that retirement can bring. However this is not the case for all older people, and many find that they are not as healthy and active as they previously were. This may result in them not being able to get about as much as they used to and they may become reliant on others for some or all of their personal care needs.

Check

- Everyone has care needs

- Everyone needs care at certain stages during their life

- People's care needs can change.

L01 Groups with personal care needs

People in wheelchairs

Some people in wheelchairs have been in a wheelchair since they were born as a result of an illness or disease. However, others use a wheelchair because of a more recent accident or illness. Many wheelchair users have to rely on others to help them with their personal care needs.

People with learning disabilities

Some people have difficulties that prevent them from learning like other people. This means they are not fully able to do everything for themselves and have to rely on others for help with their personal care needs.

Hearing impaired

Hearing impairment means a person is not able to hear sounds in the way that most of us usually do. A person may be partially hearing impaired which means they can only hear some sounds, or they may be fully hearing impaired which means they can't hear any sounds at all.

People with hearing impairment may struggle to understand instructions, which could cause problems with their personal care needs.

Visually impaired

Visual impairment means a person is not able to see as well as most people and their vision cannot be properly corrected with glasses or lenses. A person may be partially sighted, which means they can see some things, or they may be fully visually impaired which means that they can't see anything at all.

Visual impairment can make it difficult for a person to carry out some of their own personal hygiene tasks and they may need someone to help them.

People who are ill

When people are ill they may be too sick to carry out their own personal care needs and will need help and support.

Activity: How I felt when I was ill

Think back to a time when you felt unwell.

1. What could you do for yourself?

2. What could you not do for yourself?

3. Why could you not do the things you would normally do for yourself?

4. How did you feel about not being able to do things for yourself?

You may often care for someone from a different cultural background when working in health and social care

Cultural differences

There will be occasions when you will come into contact with people whose upbringing, faith, background, religion or beliefs are different from your own. These are called cultural differences. Caring for someone whose culture is different from yours does not have to be difficult and can be made easier by listening to them to learn about their care needs.

Activity: Try it for yourself

Ask a friend to blindfold you and then give you directions to follow.

1. Was this easy?

2. How did you feel when attempting the task?

3. How do you think someone who has always been visually impaired might feel if they had to do this?

4. What can be done to help visually impaired people?

Check

- There are many different groups of people with care needs

- Each group will have different needs.

L02 The personal qualities needed for personal care

Personal qualities are things about yourself that make you the person that you are.

Caring

People that receive personal care need to have it delivered to them in a very understanding manner. This means that you will need to treat service users in a way that not only meets their physical needs, but considers their emotional needs as well. You can show service users that you care by listening to them in an understanding manner.

Empathy

Empathy is about being able to understand how someone else might feel and why someone might get upset. You should try to put yourself in the position of the service user as it will help them feel that they are being listened to.

Key term

Empathy
Being able to identify with the situations of others and how they feel.

Gentleness

Care providers need to have a gentle manner and you should speak to service users in a way that is calming and supportive. There will be many times when you will need to deliver physical care to your patients. This must be done in a way that does not cause any harm or distress. Having a gentle approach will help them to trust and respect you.

Respectful

Respecting people is about valuing them for who they are and not who you think they should be.

Empowering

Empowering is about giving people choices and allowing them to use these as an opportunity to take control of their lives.

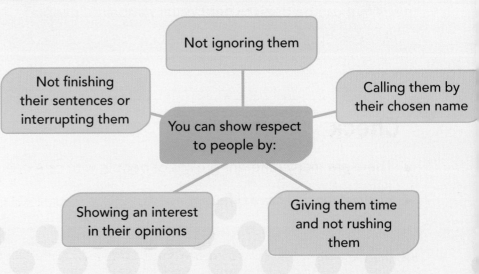

Not ignoring them

Not finishing their sentences or interrupting them

Calling them by their chosen name

You can show respect to people by:

Showing an interest in their opinions

Giving them time and not rushing them

Reliable

All care workers must be reliable. Not only must you turn up for work when you are supposed to, but you must also be trusted to do what is expected of you when you are there.

Sensitive

Care workers must treat users of services in a sensitive manner. This means in a way that does not hurt their feelings, embarrass or upset them.

Non-judgmental

Quite often people give an opinion on a person before they know anything about them. This is called being judgmental. As a care worker you must not allow your own personal opinions to get in the way of the care that you give your patients, and you must treat all of your patients in the same way.

Case study:

How should I treat you?

Barbara works at the local residential care home. She is in a hurry and is helping to feed Frank his dinner. While she is doing this, Frank keeps asking Barbara for some of his drink. Barbara refuses to give Frank a drink and tells him to be quiet and eat his dinner.

1. What is Barbara doing wrong?

2. How do you think Frank feels?

3. How do you think Barbara comes across?

4. What could Barbara do better?

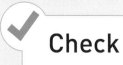

Check

- There are various different personal qualities needed to deliver care
- Care workers need to have personal qualities that show respect to the patient
- Users of services expect to be cared for in a safe and kind manner.

L02 The skills needed for personal care

How to assist with personal care

As a provider of care you will use many different skills to deliver care effectively to your patients and it is important that you do this in a way that meets the patient's needs.

Washing

Washing is important to everyone's health and wellbeing. It reduces the likelihood of you smelling of sweat, helps to remove dead skin cells from your body and also makes you feel better about yourself. Not being clean can harm people's social abilities.

Dressing

Being able to choose what to wear can be as important as being able to dress yourself. Choosing your own clothes empowers you and gives you a sense of independence. However, some people may have difficulties with putting clothes on themselves and will need assistance.

Hygienic practice

Hand washing

Here are some hand-washing tips:

- Wash hands between patients
- Wash hands before eating or touching raw foods
- Wash hands when they look dirty
- Wash hands after touching money
- Wash hands after visiting the toilet
- Wash hands before and after changing bed linen
- Wash hands before and after performing any personal hygiene tasks
- Use hot, clean water with anti-bacterial or cleansing soap
- Rub hands together thoroughly for 15–20 seconds
- Wash nails, back of hands and fingers
- Rinse hands thoroughly, removing all soap and dry hands well.

Washing your hands with soap and then using a hand santiser will ensure your hands are free from germs

How to avoid cross infection

Here are some tips to avoid **cross infection**:

- Practise good personal hygiene
- Use good cleaning practices
- Wear protective equipment, like gloves and aprons
- Use disposable tissues
- Use bins with lids
- Clean any spills immediately
- Sterilise crockery and equipment.

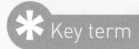

Key term

Cross infection
Transferring infection from one place to another.

How to avoid embarrassment

You can avoid embarrassing your patient by:

- Asking them what care they would like help with
- Letting them do as much as they can for themselves
- Keeping the number of people in the bathroom to a minimum
- Pulling the curtain round or closing the door
- Not getting distracted.

How to maintain privacy and dignity

You can help maintain a person's privacy and dignity by:

- Putting them first
- Giving them choices
- Listening to them
- Respecting their cultural beliefs.

How to encourage independence

You can encourage independence by:

- Allowing people to do as much as they can for themselves
- Giving them choices
- Being patient and giving them time.

Activity: Dressing difficulties

1. Why do you think some people have difficulties dressing?
2. What could you do to help someone dress?

✓ Check

- Care workers must have a range of skills to care for their patients
- Users of services are entitled to have their personal care needs met
- Care must be delivered safely and hygienically.

L02 The communication skills needed for personal care

Communication is about the giving and receiving of messages. Communicating well with others involves several different skills and involves both verbal and non-verbal messages.

Listening

Good communicators are people who listen to what the other person has to say. They pay attention to detail and observe the non-verbal messages they can hear in the person's voice. This is especially important in children as they may not be able to tell you how they are feeling. Effective listeners observe the tone, volume and speed of the person talking, and can tell if the person is angry, sad, excited or nervous.

What is this nurse doing to make it easier for the patient to hear her?

Questioning

People won't always give information to you freely. Some people don't like to be a bother and they worry that you might not be interested in what they have to say. Questioning people will make them feel that you are concerned about them and will give them the confidence to tell you how they feel. It will also give you a greater understanding of their needs, and may help you to develop a better relationship with them.

However, questioning must done in way that does not feel threatening. If you are too threatening, your patient may ignore you and never tell you how they really feel.

Non-verbal skills

Non-verbal communication is a way in which we get a message across without speaking. Examples include:

- Facial expressions – such as frowning or smiling
- Hand gestures – such as pushing away motions
- Body posture – such as leaning back and crossing arms across the chest.

Carers can use non-verbal communication skills to identify how service users are feeling.

Recording

Hand-written notes must be neat and accurate so others can clearly understand the information that has been recorded about a patient's care, and can refer back to it if they need to.

Records should contain information on:

- The patients problems
- Care needed
- Care given
- Medicines prescribed and given.

Observation

You can discover many things from watching a person, and observing your patients will help you find out what they can and can't do for themselves. As a care worker, you need to develop the skill of observation as it will tell you if your patient is scared, unhappy, worried or upset. This will help you to care for your patients better.

Case study:
Body language

Paul lives in St Andrews House Nursing Home. Most of his day is spent sat slumped in a chair watching the television in the day room. He never makes eye contact with other people and rarely talks or smiles.

1. What do you think Paul's body language says about him?

2. How do you think Paul is feeling?

3. What could you do for Paul?

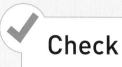

Check

- Communication is important in all care settings
- Communication involves both talking and listening.

L03 Following the health & social care setting's procedures

Moving and lifting

All organisations have procedures that they expect their staff to follow when moving and lifting, and you must not move or handle heavy objects without having correct training first. Following correct procedures reduces the chances of you injuring yourself.

Hand washing

Hand washing is the most important thing that you can do to reduce the chances of infection.

Disposal of waste

Waste produced in care settings is disposed of in a different way from the waste you produce at home. This is because a lot of the waste produced in care settings has bodily fluids on it, for example blood, urine and vomit. If it was sent to the same place as normal waste, people could be infected and the area **contaminated**.

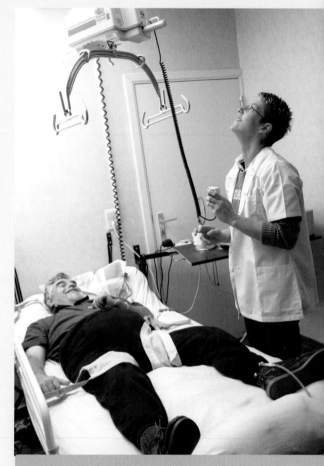

This carer is preparing to hoist the patient out of bed

Child protection

Health and social care workers have a duty to keep children safe from harm or abuse and every setting has procedures that their staff must follow. This is usually called a child protection policy. Following these procedures could prevent a child from being abused further and could help abusers to be caught.

Self protection

Some of your patients will have illnesses that may affect their memory and behaviour. This can result in service users becoming confused and they may make false claims about you and say you are doing things that you are not. If possible, it is better to have another colleague in the room.

✱ Key term

Contamination
Make unclean with a poisonous or polluting substance.

Cleaning materials

Most cleaning materials contains chemicals, because chemicals clean more effectively and help reduce the spread of infection. Therefore, cleaning materials need to be stored safely and out of the way of the service users.

Food handling

If you handle food incorrectly people can get food poisoning. Food poisoning happens when bacteria grow on food or the surfaces that the food has been prepared on. This can cause people to become sick, and in some cases, to die. Hygienic food preparation and storage practices help prevent food poisoning.

Confidentiality

All information on patients must be kept confidential and you should not pass this information on to people who do not need to know it. The reasons for this are:

- It helps patients to trust you
- It makes patients feel valued
- It makes patients feel safe
- It shows respect
- It is a legal requirement.

Case study:

Don't talk about it

Faharna works at the local nursery. While out shopping in the local supermarket, she sees one of her friends and begins to tell her about a little boy at the nursery that regularly has head lice.

1. What is Faharna doing wrong?

2. How would you expect Faharna to behave?

Check

- It is important you know what procedures are in place
- You must follow the settings procedures for giving personal care
- Following procedures will ensure high standards of care.

L03 Reasons for following the health & social care setting's procedures

Health and safety of clients

Unsafe practices can cause unnecessary harm to your patients and could make them ill. This could result in you losing your job or even being taken to court and sued.

Health and safety of carers

Your health and safety is just as important as the patients and you must not do anything that could put your health at risk. Your employer must give you a written copy of their **health and safety policy** and it is up to you to read and follow it.

Infection control

It is important for care settings to control the spread of infection within their establishments. This is so that patients do not become ill and staff and visitors do not become infected.

Efficiency

Care workers must be able to perform their job roles to the best of their abilities. This is important as settings will have limits on the number of staff they can afford to employ and will need to know that all of their service users are receiving the best care available.

Insurance

All health and social care settings must have **insurance**. This is important as it will cover them in the event of things such as:

- Fire

- Theft

- Court proceedings.

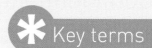
Key terms

Health and safety policy
The health and safety rules and regulations laid down by the employer.

Insurance
Money that is paid to protect in the event of something bad happening.

Regulations

Regulations are official rules or laws that say how something must be done.

Care Standards Act

The Care Standards Act is a piece of legislation (law) that sets out guidelines on the standards of care that should be provided to people who use care services. It is important in care settings as it makes service users aware of the type of care that they should expect to receive. It also ensures that all settings are giving a similar high standard of care to their service users.

National Minimum Standards in relation to personal care

The National Minimum Standards are a set of rules that apply to all care homes that provide care to older people. They include information on the quality of accommodation and personal care that service users should expect to receive. This helps carers identify how they should be giving care and makes service users aware of what care they should expect to receive.

Case study:

I have a cold

Amy-May is the receptionist at the local hospital. She has a cold and has been using disposable tissues to blow her nose. Her bin is now quite full so she empties it into a much larger bin in the back office.

1. Should Amy-May empty her bin into another?

2. Where should Amy-May empty her bin?

3. How else could Amy-May dispose of her tissues?

✓ Check

- Service users have a right to be kept safe
- Correctly following procedures can help reduce the risk of illness and injuries
- Standards of care received should be the same in all care settings.

ASSESSMENT OVERVIEW

While working through this unit, you will have prepared for completing the following assessment tasks:

○	1.1	Describe the personal care needs of individuals	Pages 62–63
○	1.2	Describe the emotional needs of individuals	Page 64–65
○	2.1	Describe the skills needed for the personal care of others	Pages 72–75
○	2.2	Describe the personal qualities needed for the personal care of others	Pages 70–71
○	3.1	Identify the health and social care setting	Pages 22–23
○	3.2	Identify the setting's procedures which relate to personal care	Pages 76–77
○	3.3	Explain why it is important to follow procedures which relate to personal care	Pages 78–79

Assignment tips

- To help you pass this unit, produce a poster that identifies and describes the personal care needs of several different users of services. Your poster should include information on the emotional needs of each of the service users you have identified.

- Produce a table listing the personal care needs of several different service users and use this to describe the personal skills and qualities needed to care for each group or individual.

- Produce a leaflet identifying a health and social care setting and giving details of the setting's procedures relating to personal care.

- The leaflet should explain why it is important to follow the procedures you have identified.

CREATIVE ACTIVITIES FOR CHILDREN

In health and social care, it is important to understand the different age groups that you may be working with.

This unit gives you an overview of the range of creative activities you can do with different age groups by focusing on children under the age of 16.

When working with different age groups, you should be aware that not all activities are suitable for all the age groups. Some creative activities, such as using scissors or needles in craft activities, may be unsafe for younger age groups, whereas other creative activities, such as finger painting, may be too basic for older children. Therefore, it is very important that you choose the right activity for the right age group.

In this unit you will:

- Learn about creative activities for children

- Carry out a creative activity with a group of children

- Look at your performance in the activity and say how you could do better

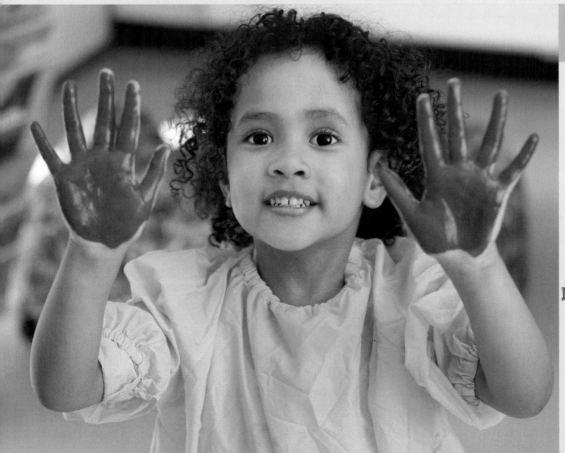

Why are creative activities great fun for children?

MidKent College
Medway Campus LRC
Medway Road
Gillingham
Kent ME7 1FN

81

L01 Know about creative activities for children

Children

When working with children you need to understand how they grow and develop. This will help you plan different activities and put out toys and equipment that will encourage children to develop physically, emotionally and socially.

0–3 years

The first year of life is one of much growth and development. Babies need adults to talk to and play with them to help their development.

Between the ages of one and three years, children love to explore objects and try to be independent. They enjoy dressing up, scribbling, playing in the sand or water pit, listening to or singing rhymes and doing general craft activities. **Creative** activities allow children to express themselves.

3–5 years

Between the ages of three and five years, children become increasingly skilled and independent. They learn many things through creative activities, for example they can learn colours by painting, and learn about writing through drawing.

! Remember

- Encourage children to do things for themselves
- Praise children when they are working well with each other
- Keep your eye on them at all times
- Provide a range of activities that will keep the children interested and help them develop different skills.

5–11 years

During these years, children's **skills** and knowledge continue to develop. By the age of 11 years, most children have a good level of reading and writing and are able to think **logically**. Children are introduced to crafts that require a little more patience and concentration, such as weaving.

* Key terms

Creative
Using the imagination to make new things.

Skill
Something that requires training or experience to do well in.

Logically
Being able to think sensibly and clearly.

Case study:

Lily

You are working with Lily who is ten years old. Her teacher has asked the class to design and draw their ideal pet. Lily has screwed her paper up and says that she cannot draw as well as her friends.

1. Why might Lily say this?

2. How would you help Lily?

11–16 years

Children at this age are going through puberty, which means that their bodies are changing and sometimes they have sudden mood swings. Creative activities help the children channel their energies. Creative activities at this stage often become a lot more focused, such as learning different drawing **techniques**.

Key terms

Technique
The way in which a task is carried out.

Manager
The person in charge of a setting or organisation.

Activity: What would you do?

You have just started your work placement at Little Acorns Nursery. The nursery has two floors. On the top floor are the children in the 0–3 years age group and downstairs are children of 3–5 years. The **manager** of the nursery has told you that today you are working upstairs and tomorrow you will be working downstairs. The manager would like you to carry out a creative activity with each age group.

1. What creative activity could you do with the 0–3 age group?
2. Why did you pick this activity?
3. What resources will you need?
4. What creative activity could you do with the 3–5 age group?
5. Why did you pick this activity?

What activites help you to relax?

✓ Check

- Babies need adults to talk and play with them
- Children try to be independent
- Creative activities are a good way to develop children's skills
- Creative activities allow children to express their thoughts and feelings.

L01 Puppets & modelling

Junk puppets and modelling

Junk puppets and junk modelling use any leftover rubbish such as egg boxes, yogurt pots and scrap materials. Children can make puppets or models that look like anything they want.

Models made from recycled materials

Key terms

Animating
To bring something to life.

Characteristics
Features or qualities that make a person recognisable.

Masks

Children like making masks as it allows them to use a variety of creative skills. Firstly they need to draw the shape and style of the mask and then add colour and detail to the mask by using various painting techniques, or maybe even printing or a collage.

Finger and hand puppets

Playing with puppets helps children in various ways, such as getting them to teach the puppet what they know. This helps children who aren't sure of themselves to feel more confident.

Finger and hand puppets are great fun to make and children enjoy **animating** puppets and giving them **characteristics**.

Play dough or clay modelling

Using play dough or clay in modelling helps develop children's **fine motor skills** and **manipulation**. Play dough is popular with children as it can be made in lots of different colours and they like the squidgy feel. The play dough can be reused, but should be changed regularly.

Clay is different as it eventually sets. Children can create a model out of the clay and then add colour to it after it has dried. Once the model is complete they may be allowed to keep the model.

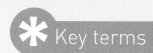

Key terms

Fine motor skills
Small movements of the hands and fingers.

Manipulation
To hold something in your hands and move it.

! Remember

- Check young children do not eat the dough
- Make sure the dough has salt in it to prevent children from eating it
- Change the dough regularly as it is handled
- Make sure children wash their hands after use.

Activity: Equipment

Make a list of all the equipment and materials you would need to carry out the following activities:

1. Making cakes out of play dough with five year olds.

2. Making finger or hand puppets with eight year olds.

3. Making animal masks for a performance of *The Jungle Book* with 15 and 16 year olds.

4. Making junk puppets or models on the theme of a farm.

✓ Check

- Making puppets and modelling develop fine motor skills and manipulation

- Making masks and models encourage a lot of other creative activities, such as drawing and painting

- Any old items can be used to make junk models and puppets.

L01 Crafts & collage

Tie and dye

Tie and dye is a fun activity to do with children and is mostly used to create unique T-shirts. The material is folded in any way that you like, and tied with string or rubber bands. The T-shirt is soaked in dye, but the ties stop the dye from colouring sections of the material.

Plaiting, twisting, knotting, weaving and stitching

These creative activities can be done in lots of different ways. Children often plait or twist their dolls' hair and they can make friendship bands out of wool or thread.

Wool or paper can be used in stitching or weaving. Children can weave simple paper baskets or make pictures by stitching. Older children may be introduced to more complex stitching with cotton and weaving with straw.

These techniques require patience and concentration, and children will need to develop independence to carry out the activities on their own.

A selection of tie-dye fabrics

Case study:

Saleem and Kevin

Saleem is enjoying making a friendship bracelet by plaiting some different coloured wool together. Kevin makes fun of Saleem and says only girls should make friendship bracelets. Saleem says he doesn't want to make them any more.

- **With a partner, think about what you would say to Saleem and Kevin.**

- **What other activities could you do with a class that involves plaiting, twisting and knotting?**

Collage

A collage is a picture made up of items stuck down. You can make a picture using cloth, pieces of paper, photographs and other objects.

Making a collage is fun for children, and it is a great way to develop their knowledge and understanding of different **textures**. You should encourage the children to think about what object best represents an item in the picture, for example children may like to use cotton wool as clouds, or lollipop sticks as a fence.

You may need to supervise the children when making a collage and give them ideas as to what objects and items they can use.

Key term

Texture
The feel and appearance of an object or surface.

Activity: What could they do?

Think about what activities the following children might enjoy doing. Record your answers on a piece of paper and feed back in a class discussion.

1. William is nine years old. Next week he is going into hospital to have an operation.

2. Rahima is 14 and is interested in becoming a fashion designer.

3. Lotti is six and wants to make something for Easter.

Functional skills

By taking part in class discussions, you will be demonstrating your English speaking and listening skills.

Check

- Collages allow children to think about different textures

- Adults should supervise children when using tie and dye, needles or making collages

- Activities must be right for the children's needs and development.

L01 Painting & printing

Painting

The type of painting that you do with the children will depend on their age. You cannot expect teenagers to enjoy finger painting or toddlers to be able to use acrylic paints.

Young children particularly like painting techniques that are fun and allow them to get messy.

Bubble painting is fun as children make the paint bubbles by blowing into straws. The imprint that the bubble makes on the paper is different every time, and children can use their imagination to describe what their pictures show.

Older children may prefer to think more about what they are actually trying to show in their paintings. They may use other **media** such as oil paints or watercolours. These allow the painters to experiment with mixing colours together.

Printing

Almost anything can be used to print with – cotton reels, corks, fruit, vegetables, hands, fingers and even feet. Printing can be used to create pictures of any kind. For example, a simple idea for autumn is creating a tree with the leaves made from handprints in a variety of orange, yellow and brown colours.

You should encourage the children to think of what items and objects would be good to use in printing and what kind of a print each will make.

Printing develops children's understanding that arts and crafts are not just about drawing and painting. They can use any item to create a picture.

✱ Key term

Medium/media
Materials used in art, such as oil paints, watercolours, pencil or collage.

Any item can be used to print with

Activity: Printing items

With a partner think about what items you could use for printing. Make a list of as many different items as you can.

Activity: Same activity, different age groups

You have finished your work placement in the nursery and you are now moving on to working in a primary school (age range 5–11 year olds) for a week and next week you will be working in a secondary school (age range 11–16 year olds). Your teacher has requested that you carry out a similar creative activity in both placements, for example printing.

1. What creative activity could you do with both age groups?

2. How would this activity differ for each age group?

3. What resources would you need for each age group?

Check

- The same activity may not be suitable for all age groups

- Children enjoy activities that meet their needs

- You can encourage children to find their own resources

- Any item can be used to create a picture.

L01 Drawing & general skills

Drawing

Drawing is a form of visual expression, and anyone can have a go at it. You can use a selection of tools and instruments to help with your drawing. The most common tool to draw with is a pencil as it is easy to remove mistakes with an eraser.

Young children like to colour in their drawings with crayons as they are soft and very colourful, whereas older children may prefer to use felt pens. These give a much sharper finish, but are hard to correct if a mistake is made.

You can encourage older children to draw with other media such as charcoals or chalks. Lessons at school or college can teach children to use a variety of drawing materials to create different pictures to help express themselves.

Case study:

Steven

Steven is a nursery assistant. He wants all the children to draw a picture of what their ideal bedroom would look like. Steven tells one girl off when she draws a slide in her bedroom as he thinks it would not work.

1. Is this a good example of a creative activity?

2. Explain your answer.

3. What could Steven have said instead?

Presenting children's work

A great way of showing the children how proud you are of their work is to display their creation in a classroom for others to see. Parents or carers as well as other children can be invited in to look at the children's creations.

Different types of paper

Paper comes in all different shapes, colours and sizes and in a variety of textures and densities. Different creative activities may require you to use different types of paper to get the finish you really want. Children particularly like using tissue paper and crepe paper. Remember to watch the children to make sure they are cutting the paper safely.

Artwork can be put on a wall-mounted display

Activity: Creative play table

You have been asked to lay out a creative play table on the theme of the beach.

1. In pairs, think of as many different things that you could put on the table that would link to this theme.

2. What would you do if a child wanted to follow a different theme?

Check

- There are lots of different tools you can use to draw with

- Drawing is a great way to express yourself

- Different paper can be used to show different textures in displays or models.

L02 Self-management & time-management

It is important to be organised when carrying out creative activities with children. You will often have to work in a group with other people and you will be expected to work together as a team.

Flexibility and responsibility

You must be **flexible** in the activities that you are in charge of. It might be that no one likes washing up the paint brushes, but you all have to take turns to do it.

You may be given the responsibility to carry out an entire activity, such as making a collage. Therefore, you may need to gather the materials and set up all the equipment before the children arrive so the activity is ready to start.

Key term

Flexible
Being able to change and adapt to different tasks and situations.

Why is it a good idea to prepare materials before the children arrive?

Case study:
Shaheen

Shaheen has worked as a nursery assistant at Hedgehogs Nursery for three years. After the children have left, the nursery assistants plan the activities for the following day. Shaheen is asked to clear up after the cutting and sticking exercise as she hasn't done any clearing up for a while. Shaheen refuses and says that she doesn't like clearing up, she likes doing fun activities with the children. The rest of the team all look annoyed.

1. Why does Shaheen's behaviour annoy the other nursery assistants?

2. What would you say to Shaheen?

Self-starting

Most of the time working with children keeps you very busy. Your placement supervisor may not have the time to keep telling you what you should do next. You need to look around your placement and see what jobs need doing without being asked.

Assertiveness

If you are **assertive**, you will stand up for your rights, but in a calm and controlled way. You won't always win, but people will know that you are a sensible person. It is not the same as aggression.

Feedback

When you have completed your creative activity, you will often receive feedback from your supervisor about how they think it went. The feedback will most likely tell you what you did well, but it will also give you ideas of what you could do better in your next activity.

Time-management is about making the most of the time you have, and planning your activities to fit in with the amount of time available.

Attendance and punctuality

Punctuality is about being on time. Arriving late (or not arriving at all) lets others down, for example it might mean that parents cannot go off to work or that others in the team have to do more than their share of work. People who are frequently late cause bad feeling in teams.

Key term

Assertive
Being confident and firm when making a point.

Remember

- Set your alarm to ensure you get up in good time
- Get enough sleep
- Leave extra time to get to work to allow for late buses or other delays
- Make sure you have all the materials needed for an activity before you carry it out.

Activity: Giving and receiving feedback

With a partner, take it in turns to say one positive and one negative thing about each other's self-management and time-management skills.

1. How will the comments you receive help you improve the way you manage yourself and your time?

2. How easy is it to give the feedback to your partner? Why?

3. How easy is it to receive the feedback from your partner? Why?

Check

- You need to be punctual when working with children
- If you cannot attend, it is important that you let others know
- Being assertive does not mean being aggressive
- Being flexible and responsible shows respect to others.

L02 Being a team member & problem solving

Carrying out creative activities with children will mean that you will often be working in a team.

Co-operating with and supporting others

Being a team member means that everyone supports each other and listens to one another. You must use your **initiative**. If you see that a member of your team is busy and a child needs help, then it is up to you to help them.

Sometimes the team will need to come together to discuss and plan the activities that they are going to do the next day. Every team member should be able to contribute to discussions, but be flexible in deciding what to do as a team.

Respecting others

Treating others with respect and courtesy helps everyone work well together.

Why is it important to work together as a team?

! Remember

- Avoid gossiping and talking about other team members
- Share ideas and take turns to do things
- Look for ways to help your team members
- Listen to others and follow instructions carefully
- Be ready to do a little more than originally planned to help others out.

Solving problems

When you carry out a creative activity, you will come across unexpected problems. How you deal with these problems can affect the overall enjoyment and success of the activity.

When you are working in the team environment, you need to be **vigilant** and look out for **potential** problems. If you see a problem, you need to think of creative ways to help solve it.

* Key terms

Initiative
Being able to act and make decisions without asking for help and advice.

Vigilant
Keeping a look out for potential problems and dangers.

Potential
Something that may be possible, but has not happened yet.

Case study:
Problem solving in a team

Students Jamelia, Lisa, Tamwar and Connor are working together in a team to organise a painting activity for 12 children in the local nursery. The group has met once to discuss what the activity will involve and to decide who will be responsible for bringing particular equipment.

On the day of the activity, Jamelia, Tamwar and Connor arrive on time, although Connor has forgotten to bring the paintbrushes. Lisa does not turn up. Connor feels really upset about forgetting the paintbrushes and so Jamelia calls a quick group meeting to discuss how they can do the activity without the paintbrushes, making sure she doesn't blame Connor. Tamwar comes up with the idea of getting the children to do finger painting instead.

The students then divide the children into four groups – something that they had planned at their meeting – and each student takes a group of children, leaving one group unsupervised.

After completing the activity, the students clear up and find that some children have got paint on the tables.

1. What problems does the group encounter?

2. Does the group spot all the problems?

3. How does the group deal with the problems?

4. Does the group work well as a team? Explain your answer.

✓ Check

- It is important for everyone to work as a team
- Good team members support each other even when things go wrong
- Sometimes you will have to do a little more than expected.

L02 Health & safety

Personal safety and others

When you are carrying out a creative activity with children, you must make sure that it is safe for everyone. If the activity involves using dangerous tools and equipment, then it may not be appropriate with a particular age group or with staff who are untrained in using the tools and equipment.

Safe use of tools

The tools that you are going to use in your activity need to be considered when you are planning the activity. Some tools can be relatively dangerous for particular groups (such as scissors), but often the children will just need supervising or assisting.

Other tools may need to be **adapted** to suit the age range and needs of the children. Needles, for example, come in different sizes including very large, blunt needles, but also small and very sharp needles.

Young children like to explore items and objects by placing them in their mouths. Ensure that any creative materials you use with young children are **non-toxic** (such as some paints and moulding dough) to avoid any problems or injuries.

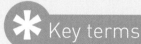 **Key terms**

Adapted
Adjusting something to meet the needs of the users of the service and the activity.

Non-toxic
Something that is not poisonous and will not cause serious harm.

! Remember

- Supervise children closely when they are using equipment such as scissors or staplers
- Avoid the use of any dangerous or unsuitable equipment
- Make sure equipment is not damaged or broken before and after use
- Make sure you know how to use the equipment safely.

📁 Case study:

Darren

Darren is on work experience in an infant school. He is carrying out a collage activity with a group of children. Darren leaves the group to cut out their materials while he goes and speaks to his friend in the class next door.

1. What could happen while Darren was gone?

2. What would you say to Darren?

Unsuitable materials

As well as picking out tools and equipment that are safe for the children to use, you will also need to consider the materials you are going to use for the activity.

Some children may have **allergies** to particular materials, such as nuts or latex in some balloons. Therefore, it is a good idea to gain a full understanding of children's medical history before using specific craft items.

Activity: Spot the hazards

Look at the picture of a nursery below.

1. Find five hazards in the picture.

2. Describe what you would do about each of the five hazards.

Check

- Activities should be safe for everyone

- Children need to be supervised when using tools

- Some activities and materials may not be safe or appropriate for every age group.

L02 Communication skills

Communication is about helping others to feel safe, involved and cared for as well as passing on information. Good communication skills help others to feel confident.

Applying literacy skills

Whether it be reading a book to a group of children, or writing their name on the back of their picture, basic **literacy** is a vital part of our day-to-day lives. Therefore, we all need to be able to read and write.

When working with children, you may be asked to produce a record of the activities that you have carried out with them. This information will need to be organised and neatly presented, giving details of each activity.

Listening and questioning skills

Listening is not the same as hearing sounds that people make when they talk. Listening skills involve hearing another person's words, thinking about what they mean and then thinking about what to say back to the other person.

A good way to show interest in what another person is saying is to ask them questions. However, you must make sure you don't ask them something that they have already told you otherwise it shows that you were not listening.

> ✱ **Key term**
>
> Literacy
> **The ability to read and write.**

Can you spot any positives with the way the adult is communicating to the child?

! Remember

- Get down to children's height
- Wait for the person to finish speaking before you speak
- Show you are listening.

Discussing activities with others

Being able to join in a discussion is an important part of any role and requires excellent listening and speaking skills. You want to show that you are interested in what others are saying, but you also need to communicate your own views and thoughts.

Activity: Listening skills

With a partner, take it in turns to talk for 30 seconds while the other ignores you.

When you have both had a go, discuss what it feels like to be the person talking, knowing that you are being ignored.

Now take it in turns to actively listen to each other and ask questions for one minute.

Discuss how it felt to be actively listened to. Is it better or worse than being ignored? Why?

Check

- Good communication skills make people confident in your ability
- It is important to listen as well as to speak
- You need to be able to communicate to run activities.

L02 Assessing own work

Assessing your work means thinking about how well you are doing. Your tutors and placement supervisors will probably tell you how you are doing. It is important to listen to them and work to improve your skills where you have weaknesses.

Strengths and weaknesses

It is easy to say what you are good at and what you think you did well, but it takes courage to admit that you are not good at some things and that you may need help to improve your performance.

If you can see your strengths and weaknesses, you will find it easier to work effectively. You need to think honestly about how you have worked and watch the reaction of the children and staff while you are working.

Constructive feedback

Your tutor and placement supervisors will be able to offer you feedback on how well they think you are getting on. They will comment on particular things you are doing well, and then give you some ideas of what you need to work on and how to improve your skills. This is called **constructive feedback**. Receiving constructive feedback is very important as it helps us to improve.

Targets

You may be set **targets** to help you to improve your performance. These will be based on your weaknesses. You will be given a date to meet the targets by, and these targets will be reviewed by your tutor or placement supervisor. At the review, they may set new targets for you or adapt the old ones.

Receiving feedback helps us to learn what skills we need to improve

* Key terms

Assessing
Judging how well you have done.

Constructive feedback
Carefully considered and useful comments to help your development.

Target
A goal to work towards.

! Remember

- Write down what you did in each activity and what happened
- Make targets that are realistic and achievable
- Check to see if you have met your targets
- If you have not met your targets, think about why.

Case study:
Assessing Lucas

Lucas enjoys going to his work placement one day a week at a primary school where he works with ages 5–11. School starts each day at 9am, but Lucas's bus doesn't arrive until 9.15am. If Lucas catches the earlier bus he is at school an hour early.

Lucas's placement supervisor, Miss Scott, has asked Lucas to carry out a creative activity with a group of learners from Reception and to carry out a creative activity with a group of learners from Year 6.

Lucas decides he will ask both groups of children to do some finger painting. He makes sure he has enough materials for all the children before he starts and explains what he would like them to do.

The children from the reception class really seem to enjoy the finger painting, whereas the children from Year 6 appear bored and start messing about. Miss Scott has to tell the children to behave.

Lucas tidies up all the paints and materials and puts them away leaving the classroom spotless.

Miss Scott has asked Lucas to assess his work. Can you help?

1. What are Lucas's strengths?

2. What are Lucas's weaknesses?

3. What targets would you set Lucas to help him improve?

Check

- Assessing your work helps you improve and develop your skills
- Be honest when thinking about your strengths and weaknesses
- Tutors and placement supervisors can help you set targets.

ASSESSMENT OVERVIEW

While working through this unit, you will have prepared for completing the following assessment tasks:

○	1.1	Describe creative activities for children aged 0–3, 3–5, 5–11, 11–16 years	Pages 82–91
○	2.1	Participate in a creative activity for children and demonstrate: • self-management skills • a positive contribution as team member • meeting agreed deadlines • problem-solving skills • safe practice • communication skills	 Pages 92–93 Pages 94–95 Pages 92–93 Pages 94–95 Pages 96–97 Pages 98–99
○	3.1	Assess own work-related skills in supporting children's creative activities	Pages 100–101

Assignment tips

- To help you pass this unit, you could produce a nursery and school floor plan with pictures and titles of a number of creative activities for children.

- Make sure your activities are varied and that you have activities that are suitable for different age groups with different needs.

- When carrying out an activity, make sure you take an active part and show what you can do.

- Make a checklist of what materials you need, who is responsible for what, and what time you need to be there.

- Remember to listen carefully to instructions and co-operate as a member of the team.

- Keep a diary or otherwise record all the activities you do and what your role was in each activity.

- Get tutors or other helpers to sign your record to confirm what you did in the activity.

- Ask them to comment on how well you did these jobs. Using this feedback, make a list of areas where you need to do better and explain why.

LEARNING EXPERIENCES FOR CHILDREN & YOUNG PEOPLE

There are several learning experiences that children of all ages can be involved in. These experiences help children to grow and develop and it is important that you are aware of the different activities that are appropriate for children in each age range.

This unit looks at a variety of different learning experiences available to children and young people. It also aims to encourage the skills that are essential for providing these experiences, and ways you can assess your own work-related skills when providing activities.

In this unit you will:

● Learn about different types of play for children and young people

● Explore work-related skills required when providing learning experiences for children and young people

● Understand how to assess your own work-related skills when providing learning experiences for children and young people

Think about how children learn through play.

L01 Know about learning experiences 0–3 years

There is a variety of activities and experiences that we can provide for children and young people that will help them grow and learn.

Children within the 0–3 years age range learn through moving around and using their senses – hearing, seeing, touching, smelling and tasting.

Books and stories

Reading is an important part of everyday life and children should be introduced to reading from a very early age. Stories are imaginative accounts of events or happenings. However, at this age, books and stories need to be short because children are unable to concentrate for very long.

Rhymes

Rhymes are short stories using words that sound similar to each other. Rhymes are a good way of keeping children's interest and helping them to learn and develop language skills.

Soft books are an ideal way to introduce babies to reading

Music, singing and moving

Music and singing give children the opportunity to experiment, use their imagination and develop basic words. Listening to music can encourage children to sit still and concentrate on what is being said to them. It can also be an effective way of keeping them interested, as children often enjoy moving around and keeping in time to music.

Treasure baskets and household utensils

A treasure basket is a container of everyday items, for example, necklaces, teaspoons or shells. The use of these and other household objects help children learn about the world around them at a basic level.

Playing with a pram

When a child starts to walk they begin to use their imagination in new ways. Playing with a pram encourages children to learn how to care for others.

Bath toys

Bath toys encourage young children to enjoy the bath-time experience. This will also help them develop good hygiene from a very early age.

Games

Games help develop social skills. These skills should be introduced from a very young age as it will help children learn to play together.

Peek-a-boo

Peek-a-boo is a game of hide and seek using the hands and encourages interaction and facial expressions.

Table-top games

At this age table-top games can include matching games and pairs where children learn how to sit still and take turns with other children. They also help develop their memory skills.

Outdoor activities

Outdoor activities encourage children to learn about the wider world around them. They help them to develop physical skills and can encourage them to burn off energy.

- *Parks* have space for children to run around
- *Shops* allow children to see and hear many things
- *The seaside* has many different exciting sights, sounds and textures.

Activity: Activities suitable for under 3s

In pairs, make a poster that shows several different examples of activities that babies and young children enjoy. Remember to use pictures and images to make your poster interesting.

Functional skills

By making a poster, you will be demonstrating your **English** writing skills.

Check

- There is a range of learning experiences for children age 0–3 years
- All babies and children enjoy being involved in learning activities.

L01 Know about learning experiences 3–5 years

As children get older, their learning experiences need to be more challenging to help them grow and develop.

Books

Books for children within this age range need to be simple picture-style books that have bold, attractive images. Any text should be large, simple and easy to understand.

Stories

Reading stories to children in this age range helps them to learn new words and can make a child feel loved and cared for.

Rhymes and poems

Learning rhymes and poems helps children to explore sounds. It encourages them to develop memory and language skills, which will help them with the first stages of reading.

Singing, listening and moving to music

Children enjoy being involved in music and singing activities. It develops their language skills and can help them to express themselves and concentrate.

Children enjoy music and learning to play instruments

Games

Children now start playing alongside others. They watch carefully what other children are doing and begin to join in simple games.

Jigsaw puzzles and table-top games

Jigsaw puzzles and table-top games can be used to encourage children to build up certain skills, for example:

- Learning to share
- Taking turns
- Co-operating with others
- Developing hand-to-eye co-ordination.

Computer software

There are a number of computer games aimed at teaching children of this age group. Computer software needs to be chosen carefully, and good games can help develop children's education in many ways, such as:

- Developing reading skills
- Helping with basic maths
- Learning about colour and shapes.

Outdoor activities

Outdoor activities for young children can be fun and healthy. Children love to explore outdoors. However, they must be supervised at all times at this age and any activities should be managed in a safe and secure environment.

Gardening

At this age children can be involved in simple gardening activities. Planting seeds, such as cress and beans will help children learn how to care for the things around them.

Ball games

Balls games are an excellent way for children to exercise. They help with hand-to-eye co-ordination and arm movements.

Kites

Children love to fly kites. However, making kites can be as much fun as flying them.

Cooking and baking

Children love to cook and bake things. Cooking can be introduced at this age through toys, such as kitchens, pots and pans and play food.

Functional skills

By producing a leaflet, you will be demonstrating your **English** writing skills.

Activity: What type of play?

Produce a leaflet that describes different types of learning experiences appropriate for children age 3–5 years.

Remember to make your leaflet colourful and eye-catching by including pictures and images.

Check

- Play helps babies and young children learn
- Learning experiences change as children get older.

L01 Know about learning experiences 5–11 years

Children at this stage have developed their social skills much further. This means that they will play quite happily with other children and will identify one or two favourite friends that they want to play with.

Books and magazines

Use books and magazines to develop their reading skills choosing ones that have more difficult words.

Poems

At this age, children will often be interested in writing poems for themselves. This is readily encouraged within the school curriculum and helps children to develop their language skills further.

Singing, listening and dancing to music

The use of musical instruments is encouraged within the school curriculum and a lot of children at this age become interested in playing a proper musical instrument.

They have developed a much stronger sense of melody and will use this to join in with singing and dancing to music.

Table-top games

Table-top games for children within this age range need to be more complex. By now they have a better understanding of sharing and will enjoy the competitive nature of most table-top games.

Floor games

Floor games help children within this age range to develop both physically and mentally. Floor games give children exercise and encourage them to share and work with each other. Examples include:

- Hopscotch
- River stones
- Stepping stones
- Patterned and numbered floor mats
- Skipping.

Children enjoying hopscoch together

Computer software

Computer software for children within this age range needs to be challenging enough to prevent boredom. Computer software helps with hand-to-eye co-ordination and also can promote fine motor skills.

Outdoor activities

Children's health is promoted by being involved in outdoor activities.

Pavement games

Pavement activities can help a child's imagination as they will make up games that they can play with others.

Ball games

These help to develop a child's co-ordination and communication skills.

Cooking and baking

Older children love to experiment with cooking and baking. Children will gain valuable life skills from cookery and satisfaction from eating something they have produced.

Case study:
What shall I do?

Jacqueline lives in a block of flats and does not have access to a garden of her own. She does not enjoy staying indoors and therefore plays with other children on the streets near to her home.

1. **Describe different learning experiences Jacqueline can be involved in with her friends in the street?**

2. **List the equipment needed for each learning experience.**

Check

- Learning activities can encourage children to share and co-operate with others

- Some learning experiences are linked to the school curriculum.

L01 Know about learning experiences 11–16 years

Young people at this age mix very well with others of similar ages. Boys and girls are happy to mix with each other and begin to develop deep, lasting friendships.

Music

Many older children have by now developed a strong sense of beat and rhythm and they use this to inform the types of music they prefer. Most are now listening to the **lyrics** that are being sung and will have a greater understanding of the messages that the musicians are trying to get across. They have also developed a preference for particular types of music.

Dance

There are a variety of dance classes available for children. They give children the opportunity to keep fit and exercise. Dance also helps with confidence building and encourages concentration. Examples of dance classes include:

- Ballet
- Jazz
- Street dance
- Hip hop
- Tap
- Modern
- Ballroom
- Irish.

Young people of this age enjoy going to clubs aimed specifically at their own age groups, to socialise and dance with their friends.

Exercise

Exercise is important for children at any age. However, children grow rapidly within this age group and the onset of **puberty** can cause many physical and emotional changes. Exercise can help to reduce any stress that this may cause.

Yoga

Yoga is an ancient form of exercise that originated in India. It helps with flexibility and can strengthen and tone muscles.

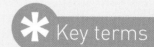
Key terms

Lyrics
Words of a song.

Puberty
The stage when a boy or girl becomes sexually reproductive.

Computers

Computers are used in almost every part of the modern world. Therefore, it is important that children have learning experiences that involve the use of them. Children within this age range can work well with computers and the use of them will help challenge and stimulate their ever-increasing skills and knowledge.

Children are often taught IT at school

Graphics

Graphics are visual forms of presenting things on a surface, such as canvas, computer screens and paper. Examples of graphics include:

- Photographs
- Drawings
- Pictures
- Tables

- Graphs
- Maps
- Diagrams.

They can help promote and develop artistic abilities and IT skills in older children.

Electronic games

Older children and young people enjoy activities that involve the use of electronic equipment. Electronic games are an excellent source of entertainment and can be a stimulating way for children within this age range to learn.

Activity: What I liked to do

1. Make a list of all the activities you enjoyed when you were 11–16 years old.

2. Explain why you liked doing these activities.

3. What do you think you learned from these experiences?

Check

- Older children still enjoy being involved in learning experiences

- Exercise is important for children of all ages and reduces emotional stress.

L02 Self-management

Planning learning experiences for children and young people takes a lot of preparation, and there are many skills that you need to have to do this effectively.

When working within care settings, it is vital that you demonstrate good **self-management skills**. These involve being able to make choices and decisions for yourself.

Flexibility

You need to be able to show that you can be flexible within your working day. This could be in relation to the tasks that you are asked to carry out, but may well include your working times and patterns.

Taking responsibility

During the working day you will be expected to take responsibility for what you do, or do not do. It is important that you take responsibility for any activities that you have been asked to carry out.

Gathering materials, setting up and tidying up

Before you begin any activity, it is up to you to ensure that you have all the correct equipment ready. Children will be more likely to join in if your activity is set up attractively, and you should lay everything out in a way that gets the children's attention.

Clearing away properly is as vital as setting up correctly. Some activity pieces can cause potential hazards if they are left out where children can get to them unsupervised.

Try to get the children to join in packing away

Self-starting

You must be able to show that you can get on with tasks without prompting from other members of staff. **Self-starters** do the following:

- Look for tasks to get on with
- Take responsibility for themselves.
- Finish tasks they start

Key term

Self-starting
The ability to show that you can get on with tasks without prompting.

Assertiveness

It is important that you assert yourself when working with children. You can show assertiveness by speaking in a confident manner and sticking to what you have said, but not becoming aggressive.

Readiness to improve own performance based on feedback

After carrying out activities it is important that you get feedback on your performance. Feedback can help you to improve your performance and you must be prepared to gather feedback and use it.

Case study:

Tidy up!

Bradley has been doing a painting activity with a small group of children. At the end of the activity, he tells the children that they can go and play outside once everything has been cleared up and packed away. He gives each child a task to do and supervises and praises them while they are clearing up.

1. Explain why children should pack away after themselves.

2. How will praising the children help?

3. What else could Bradley do to encourage the children to help clear up?

✓ Check

- There are many skills you need to have to work with young people
- You must be willing to continually improve your own performance.

L02 Being a team member & time management

It is important that you develop skills in working with others and becoming an effective team member. Employers want team members to:

- Have a good attitude
- Be willing to help out
- Be flexible
- Be reliable
- Be happy and positive
- Co-operate with others
- Communicate and share information freely with other team members.

Respecting, supporting and co-operating with others

While in the working environment you need to show that you respect and value others around you. There will be many times when you have to co-operate and help others out. This is important for building professional relationships. You can show that you respect someone by doing the following things:

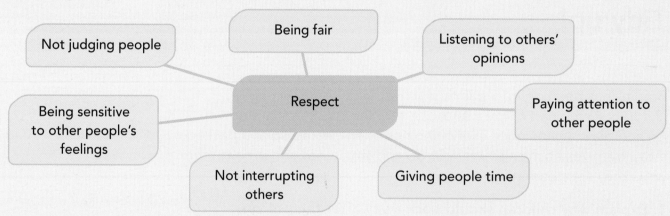

Negotiating and persuading

Negotiating involves being able to talk about something and then agreeing an outcome that suits everyone, whereas persuading involves being able to convince others to your point of view.

Contribution to discussions

You must be able to communicate effectively when caring for others. This means joining in conversations at appropriate times and making sensible comments.

Awareness of interdependence on others

There will be many times when you have to rely on the support and assistance of others to fulfil your duties. This means you must learn how to interact and co-operate with other team members.

Attendance and punctuality

It is important that you go to work when you should do. If you are absent from work, your colleagues will have to complete some of your work as well as their own. Regular attendance at work shows:

- Commitment to the job
- Concern for others
- **Conscientiousness.**

You are expected to report to work on time everyday. Lateness causes resentment and can damage the relationships that you have with your colleagues.

Key term

Conscientiousness
Doing things properly and correctly.

Completing task within agreed time frame

While at work you will be given tasks to carry out within certain time frames. You must demonstrate that you can complete these duties within the agreed times.

Activity: I'm late

Sonny works at the local nursery. The bus he catches to work arrived early and he has missed it. It is the third time this week that Sonny is late.

1. Whose fault is it that Sonny is late for work?
2. How could Sonny's lateness impact on his co-workers?
3. How do you think Sonny's colleagues might feel about Sonny being late so often?
4. What can Sonny do to make sure he is on time for work?

Check

- Team work is important
- It is important that you support and respect others
- Adults that work with children must be reliable and punctual
- You must complete work within agreed time frames.

L02 Communication skills & problem solving

To work effectively you need to demonstrate effective communication skills. Communication involves getting messages across and this can be done in many ways, for example:

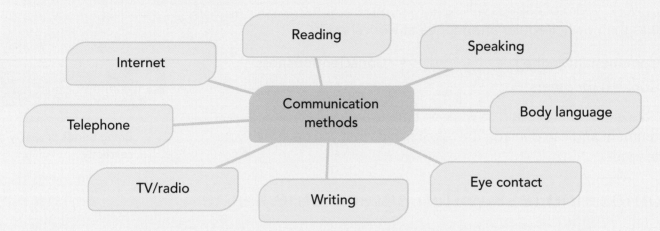

Applying literacy skills

Literacy skills are what we need to read and write effectively. There will be many times when you will have to read and write about users of services and their care needs and it is vital that the information you gather and pass on is accurate.

Producing clear and accurate records of activities

Recording activities provides written evidence of a person's progress and can help identify any gaps in their learning. You should write clearly, without spelling errors, and keep records in a safe place.

Listening and questioning skills

It is important that you can listen and question effectively.

Listening	Questioning
Shows you are paying attention	Shows you are actively listening
Builds a rapport with others	Helps to gather additional information
Shows support	Demonstrates understanding and interest
Helps discover things that are going on	Shows you are interested

Discussing activities with colleagues, tutors, children

Communicating with others is an important part of your job role and you will need to show that you can talk to individuals and groups of people of varying ages and levels.

Identifying a problem

Before you can begin the process of **problem solving**, you need to be able to identify the problem. This can be done by writing the problem down and identifying where it is and what is causing it. Problems often occur as a result of:

- *Lack of materials*: there are not enough for everyone to use
- *Materials will not work*: equipment is broken or damaged.

You will need to show that you can offer sensible solutions to solve the problems you have identified.

Creative thinking

Creative thinking is about coming up with new ideas. A creative thinker:

- Invents different ways of doing things
- Has original ideas
- Encourages people to alter their way of thinking.

Activity: Was it clear?

1. Produce a written account of an activity that you have done.
2. Ask someone to read what you have written.
3. Are they able to understand what you are describing?
4. Ask them to explain to you how well you have written the account of the activity.

Check

- It is important that you can communicate well with others
- You must produce and keep accurate records
- You should be able to identify problems and think of ways to solve them.

Key term

Problem solving
The process of finding an answer or solution to a problem.

Functional skills

By writing an account of your activity, you will be demonstrating your English writing skills.

L02 Health & safety and application of IT

It is important to ensure a safe environment for children and young people.

Outdoor equipment

All outdoor equipment needs to be checked to make sure it is safe to use and there are no missing, sharp or broken pieces that could harm children.

Children working in groups

Working with others can be a fun and enjoyable learning experience for children. However, you need to ensure that this is done safely.

What can you do to create a safe environment for children and babies?

Taking risks in a safe environment

Children need to understand risks and be guided to play in a safe environment.

Basic IT skills

Computers are a huge part of everyday life therefore it is important that you have good IT skills.

Basic IT skills include things like being able to turn a computer on and off correctly, use a mouse, use a keyboard and open and use applications safely.

Use of Word and email

Word is an application found on most computer systems which you can use to produce written information and documents. Email is a form of communication that can be used to send and receive information to others instantly.

Use of internet search engines

Internet search engines are rapidly becoming excellent ways to source information on the world wide web and you need to be able to demonstrate that you are able to research and gather information in this manner.

Identifying resources

Identifying resources needed for any activities you wish to carry out should be done as part of the planning stage of your activity.

Ideas

Children like to be involved in activities, but they can become bored very easily. Therefore, it is important that you try to come up with ideas on different activities that the children will enjoy.

Safe practice

You must ensure the safety of the users of services that are in your care at all times. This means looking out for and identifying any potential **hazards** that could harm them and taking reasonable steps to reduce the **risk** of this happening.

Key terms

Hazard
Anything that could potentially cause harm to someone.

Risk
The chances of a hazard causing harm.

Activity: Spot the hazards

1. Produce a plan of an indoor play area. Within your plan include:

   - Toys and play equipment
   - Plug sockets and light switches
   - Toilets and washing facilities
   - Kitchen and eating areas
   - Quiet/reading corners.

2. On a separate piece of paper identify anything within your plan that could be a hazard to the children.

3. Explain why you think these may be hazards.

Check

- Children expect adults to keep them safe
- Computers are used in many parts of our lives.

L03 Assessing own work

You must be able to assess your own work. This will help you to find out about your progress so far and discover how others view your work-related skills.

Constructive feedback from colleagues/tutor/line manager

Constructive feedback from others can help develop our working practice. Feedback helps boost a person's self-esteem and confidence, and encourages good working surroundings.

Formal feedback

Formal feedback is usually given to you in a planned and official manner. Examples include:

- **Appraisals** with your line manager
- Written observations
- Discussions after a particular job or task
- Feedback from an unsuccessful job interview.

Informal feedback

Informal feedback is given to you in a casual manner. Examples include:

- Casual discussions at the end of a day
- Chats with your colleagues during breaks
- Positive comments made throughout the working day.

Areas of strength and weakness

You must be able to identify your strengths and weaknesses in order to progress. Being aware of what you do well can improve your self-esteem and confidence, whereas being aware of the things that you cannot do so well, will enable you to practise and improve on them.

Feedback from colleagues can often be informal.

✳ Key term

Appraisal
Formal assessment of your work.

Setting targets for further development

Once your areas of strength and weakness have been identified, you should use this information to set yourself targets to improve your development further.

Targets are goals that you set with sensible timescales. When setting targets, you must ensure you are clear about what you want to achieve, for example:

- Get a qualification
- Develop communication skills
- Improve IT skills.

All targets you set yourself must be *SMART*. This means they are:

- *Specific*: you must know exactly what you want to achieve
- *Measurable*: you must know when you have met the target
- *Achievable*: you must be able to successfully achieve the target
- *Realistic*: the target set must be a thing that can be done
- *Time*: you must give yourself enough time to meet your target.

Activity: My strengths and weaknesses

1. Produce a table similar to the one below that you can use to identify your strengths and weaknesses.

Strengths	Weaknesses
Good time keeper	*Lack IT qualifications*
Communicate well with peers	*Struggle to communicate with senior staff*

2. Using the information you have gathered above, describe with examples things you can do to improve your weak areas.

Check

- It is important that you assess your own work-related skills
- Assessing your work-related skills will help you identify things that you do well and improve any weak areas in your development
- Constructive feedback is an important process of discovering gaps in skills and knowledge.

ASSESSMENT OVERVIEW

While working through this unit, you will have prepared for completing the following assessment tasks:

○	1.1	Describe learning experiences for children and young people aged 0–3, 3–5, 5–11, 11–16 years	Pages 104–111
○	2.1	Participate in a learning experience for children or young people and demonstrate:	
		• self-management skills • a positive contribution as a team member • meeting agreed deadlines • problem-solving skills • safe practice • communication skills • the use of IT	Pages 112–113 Pages 114–115 Pages 114–115 Pages 116–117 Pages 118–119 Pages 116 –117 Pages 118–119
○	3.1	Assess own work-related skills required for providing learning experiences for children and young people	Pages 120–121

Assignment tips

- To help you pass this unit, you could produce a table that describes some learning experiences suitable for children and young people for each age group.

- The table can also include a column describing the resources needed for each learning experience, with additional information explaining any health and safety issues that might be involved.

- You could participate in work experience in an early years setting and get a witness testimony completed by staff on their work-related skills.

- Additionally, you could work in small groups and produce presentations on learning experiences for children and young people. This can then be used to demonstrate your work-related skills.

- Your colleagues can give you feedback on presentations/group work in relation to work-related skills, and you can then use this to identify your strong and weak areas. This information can then be used to produce a realistic plan on how to improve your performance.

CREATIVE & LEISURE ACTIVITIES FOR ADULTS IN HEALTH & SOCIAL CARE

Creative and leisure activities cover a huge range of interests and pastimes to suit individuals. Creative activities could include hobbies such as sketching and knitting whereas examples of leisure activities could be swimming or reading.

When working with different client groups, you should realise that not all activities are suitable for all the clients because of their abilities and disabilities.

This unit explores the range of activities that could be carried out with adults while investigating their suitability for particular groups and needs.

In this unit you will:

- Learn about creative and leisure activities for adults

- Carry out a creative or leisure activity with a group of adults

- Look at your performance in the activity and say how you could do better

What benefits do creative and leisure activities provide for adults?

L01 Creative & leisure activities for adults

Adults who use health and social care services are quite likely to have difficulties or disabilities of some kind. These factors need to be considered before planning any creative or **leisure** activities.

Physical difficulties, mental health and frailty

As we get older, our bodies start to **deteriorate** and can leave us in a state of **frailty** with poor hearing or vision. We can forget things that have happened in our lives and find it difficult to concentrate.

Our bones and joints can also start to get weak and can break easily or get really stiff, making it hard to move around. Some adults get **arthritis** which causes swelling and stiffness in joints, muscles and bones and can make moving extremely painful.

Sometimes we can lose our ability to manipulate objects with our hands and fingers due to problems with our joints and bones.

Learning disabilities

A learning disability can make it harder for some people to learn, understand and communicate. This is because disability can slow down the learning and development abilities of the brain. It can affect skills including the ability to speak, listen, understand, read and write.

People with learning disabilities may need full-time help to cope with every day activities including eating, drinking, washing, dressing and toileting.

✳ Key terms

Leisure
Free time to enjoy a hobby or relaxing activity.

Deteriorate
To slowly get worse.

Frailty
When someone is weak and their bones break easily.

Arthritis
A medical condition that causes pain in joints, muscles and bones.

What creative and leisure activities do you think these adults would enjoy?

Ill health

Being in ill health means different things to different people and it affects us all in different ways. A common cold may affect you differently from your friend. You may feel you need to stay in bed and get better, whereas your friend may feel that they are able to go to work.

! Remember

- Look at the needs of your client groups and pick an activity according to their needs
- Supervise more vulnerable groups and groups that are using dangerous tools
- Encourage adults to join in creative and leisure activities.

◎ Activity: Choosing an activity

1. In pairs or small groups, discuss why you have to think about each factor listed below when you are planning an activity for adults.

   - Physical difficulties
   - Learning disabilities
   - Ill health
   - Mental health
   - Frailty.

2. What problems could you encounter as a result of these factors?

Functional skills

By taking part in a discussion, you will be demonstrating your English speaking and listening skills.

✓ Check

- Adults using health and social care settings are likely to need help
- Our health deteriorates as we get older
- We can lose the ability to do certain things as we get older
- Being ill affects everyone differently.

125

L01 Creative activities

Drawing, painting and photography are great creative activities to carry out with adults. You can do them anywhere, and you can draw, paint or photograph anything.

If an individual is **housebound**, they can draw, paint or photograph objects and items in their own home. If they are able to get out, then trips to the countryside or the beach can be arranged to stimulate ideas of things to draw, paint and photograph.

Key term

Housebound
When someone cannot leave their house.

Painting

Some particular groups of adults will enjoy basic painting techniques and blending colours together. Other groups will prefer to use more developed techniques, such as using oil paints or watercolours.

Some adults may attend specialised classes in learning how to paint with watercolours, or alternatively a regular painting session may be held in a health and social care setting to provide stimulation and encourage the adults to be creative.

Drawing

A good thing about drawing is that anyone can have a go at it. It doesn't matter whether you think you are good or bad. It is a form of visual expression.

You can use a selection of tools to help with your drawing. The most common tool is a pencil. Other popular drawing tools include charcoal, pastels and inks.

Why is it good for older adults to attend drawing classes?

Photography

Photography is a lovely way of showing how a person views the world. Photographs can capture the mood of the photographer and the **atmosphere** of what they are photographing. Individuals can **reveal** their thoughts through their work.

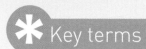

Key terms

Atmosphere
The mood and feeling of something.

Reveal
To show something that was unclear.

! Remember

- Check camera for film and batteries (if film camera)
- Check camera for SD card and batteries (if digital camera).

Case study:

Lenny

Lenny is a 36-year-old man who has Down's Syndrome. He visits a day care centre every week. The day care centre allows Lenny to take part in a range of creative activities, and he really enjoys photography. He enjoys taking pictures of animals. Recently a new member of staff has started working at the centre and has told Lenny that he is not allowed to do photography any more as he 'isn't very good at it, as the only things he takes pictures of are animals'. Since the new member of staff said this, Lenny hasn't visited the day care centre.

With a partner, discuss the following questions:

1. **Why do you think Lenny stops attending the day care centre?**

2. **Is the new member of staff correct in stopping Lenny from doing photography?**

3. **Does it matter that Lenny only takes pictures of animals? Why?**

✓ Check

- Painting, drawing and photography can be enjoyed anywhere
- Painting, drawing and photography allow the artists to show their feelings
- Anyone can have a go at painting, drawing and photography.

L01 Other creative activities

There are many other creative activities that adults can enjoy apart from drawing and painting.

Drama

Drama can help adults to build relationships with one another and **enhance** communication skills. Drama doesn't always mean being given a particular role to play. It could be expressing yourself through your understanding of objects and situations.

Pottery/clay modelling

Adults enjoy pottery as they can make objects and items that they can keep or give to others as presents. Pottery and modelling also gives adults the chance to glaze or paint their creation once it has been fired. Pottery and modelling can benefit adults as they have to use their skills of manipulation.

Sewing and knitting

Sewing is the making of things with fabric, using needles and thread. This can include clothes, or other household items such as curtains and cushions.

Anyone can take part in a creative or leisure activity.

Another form of sewing is to use patterns to create pictures. Cross-stitch is a popular pastime as you do not have to have any experience in sewing to be able to complete the pattern.

Some adults also enjoy knitting as you can create a variety of items such as clothes or toys. Knitting can help concentration and also enhance fine motor skills.

! **Remember**

- Provide a range of activities that will keep the adults interested
- Check how many people would like to take part in the activity before you start
- Check you have enough materials and tools
- Clear up fully, putting everything away tidily for the next use.

Weaving

Weaving is the art of crossing two sets of materials over and under each other. It requires a lot of patience and can take a long time. Basic weaving can create items that are flat and small, such as a drinks mat. Weaving can be done on a much a larger scale, creating blankets or baskets.

Case study:

New activities

A residential home is looking for some new creative activities to do with the residents. They often do drawing and painting, but they would like to do something a bit different.

The staff are concerned as the following residents have particular needs:

Doreen is quite shy and likes to be left alone. Ravi has dementia and can quickly forget what he is doing. Samuel has arthritis in his hands and struggles to bend his fingers. Sang-mi has a visual **impairment** making her sight very poor.

The manager of the home asks you for help. In small groups, answer the following questions.

1. **What activities would you suggest the home does?**
2. **Are all the activities suitable for each resident? If not, why?**
3. **What problems might the staff face?**

 **Key term**

Impairment
The loss of normal function of part of the body due to disease or injury, such as loss of eyesight.

 ## Activity: What's on?

Find out what creative activities are available for adults in your local area. You could look on the internet, in your local newspaper, magazines and *Yellow Pages*.

 # Check

- Drama helps people to communicate
- Creative activities help improve concentration and patience
- Adults can feel a sense of satisfaction on seeing their creation.

L01 Leisure activities

Reading

Losing yourself in a book is a very relaxing pastime as you can imagine the characters and events in the book. Adults can enjoy reading by themselves and this will help to stimulate their **imagination**.

Reading a book to a group of adults can be enjoyable as you can show the emotions and mood of the book through facial expressions and tone. Some adults who cannot read may enjoy having books read to them.

Games

Playing games like board games or card games helps to keep the mind active. Games such as word or number puzzles can be played by individuals, others can be played in a group, for example bingo.

There is a variety of game shows and quizzes on television, which adults can watch and join in with at home. Some games can be played on the computer and on the internet.

Games can be cheap if they are homemade, for example word searches or crossword puzzles.

Music

Listening to music can be done individually or in a group. It can be relaxing and calms adults when they are feeling stressed, or it can be used to animate adults.

Instruments can be used to play along to the music, or simply to create your own music. Adults could have fun making the instruments first and then playing them.

Cooking

This is a good way to allow adults to be creative and achieve a sense of **satisfaction** when they eat their end product. You could choose something simple to cook to start with, such as cakes or biscuits, or make a group activity such as cooking a meal.

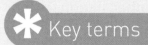

* Key terms

Imagination
Thinking of ideas and images in the mind.

Satisfaction
Feeling pleased and happy with achievements.

How can you make cooking fun?.

! Remember

- Check you have all the ingredients before you start
- Check the surfaces are clean to work on
- Make sure everyone has washed their hands
- Make sure anyone with loose hair has tied it back
- Wear aprons to protect your clothes.

Case study:
New activities

Elise is 28 and has a physical disability that stops her from walking without the use of a walking frame.

Elise lives alone in a two-bedroom bungalow with no family nearby. She likes listening to stories and playing games on her computer. Elise used to go to the local leisure centre, but as she has no transport, she no longer goes. She really misses the new friends that she made there.

1. **Suggest three leisure activities that Elise might enjoy.**

2. **Suggest ways that Elise could still keep in contact with her new friends.**

3. **What leisure activities could Elise do in her own home with her friends?**

✔ Check

- Reading stimulates the imagination
- Games can keep the mind active and develop confidence
- Cooking gives individuals a sense of reward when they eat their creation
- Music can be relaxing or stimulating.

L01 Physical leisure activities

Exercise

It is recommended that we all have 30 minutes of exercise every day, such as a brisk walk. For some adults a brisk walk may not be possible, but there are other forms of exercise that can be tried.

Adults that have mobility problems can exercise in a chair by carrying out a range of movements with their arms and legs. This can help their muscles and joints. Other adults may prefer to go for a swim.

Don't assume that particular adults cannot do certain activities.

! Remember

- **Choose exercise activities that are suited to the needs and abilities of the individuals**
- **Supervise more strenuous and dangerous activities**
- **Avoid planning an exercise activity for a long period of time.**

Gardening/growing

Gardening and growing can provide a real sense of satisfaction as you are rewarded for your hard work in the form of flowers and food.

Gardening and growing plants requires a lot of patience and effort and is a continual job as the plants need to be watered and kept free of weeds.

Adults in health and social care settings could be given a specific place of their own such as a small part of a garden where they could grow their own flowers and plants. Alternatively, adults could work together to maintain and grow an area.

Outings

Taking adults out in society is a key part of maintaining and enhancing their **social skills**. An outing could be a trip to the theatre or the cinema or a meal in a local pub or restaurant.

Bingo is also a popular outing as it encourages adults to play a game, to stimulate their memory skills and improve their **reactions**.

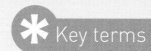

Key terms

Social skills
Being able to interact effectively with others.

Reaction
A response to something.

Activity: Helping adults to choose an activity

These adults want to do a leisure activity, but are unsure of what activity to pick. Read the statements made by the adults and choose a leisure activity suitable for them.

1. Carlo: 'I want to get fit, but I'm scared of water.'

2. Monique: 'I like to get outside and potter about.'

3. Adrian: 'I want an activity that will take a long time to complete.'

4. Trish: 'I want to meet other people.'

5. Pavel: 'I like to do leisure activities on my own.'

Check

- Exercise helps to keep our bodies fit and healthy
- Gardening and growing develops patience and ownership
- Outings can help adults improve their social skills.

L02 Self-management & time-management

Flexibility

A lot of adults that use health and social care services need full-time help and support. This means that they may need someone to be with them 24 hours a day. As no one can be expected to work 24 hours a day, you may be required to work shifts.

Working shifts requires you to be flexible and work at different times of the day. You may have to work nights too.

Case study:

Shift patterns

Kristina has recently got a job as a care worker in a nursing home. She has been given her rota telling her when she will be working. She is due to work some nights and some days. On Kristina's first night, she falls asleep. The manager tells Kristina off for falling asleep.

1. **Why do you think Kristina's manager is angry that Kristina falls asleep?**

2. **Why is it important that Kristina stays awake?**

3. **What advice could you give Kristina?**

Taking responsibility and being self-starting

When you are working with adults in health and social care, there will be times when you will need to use your initiative to help out. It may be that your placement supervisor is busy and hasn't given you any jobs to do. Rather than just waiting for instructions, you should look for things that need doing or that will help the people in your care.

Case study:

Using your initiative

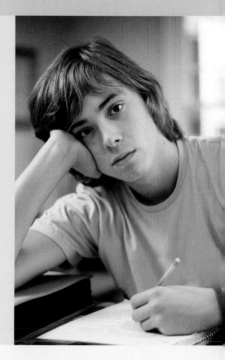

Jonas is a work experience learner on a work placement at a day care centre for older people. When Jonas's tutor from college comes to visit, Jonas tells her that the placement is really boring and the older people don't do anything. Jonas says that the staff keep giving him instructions, but when he has finished his task he has nothing else to do.

The placement supervisor says that Jonas just stands around looking bored. They try to encourage him to get involved, by asking him to do particular tasks, but when he finishes them, he just stands around.

The users of the service would like to play games and chat to people, but the staff are quite busy and don't have time to do it.

1. What advice would you give Jonas?

2. What advice would you give the placement supervisor?

Attendance and punctuality

Being on time when working with adults is very important. If you are late, it may mean that an adult with specific needs is left uncared for. If you are frequently late, the users of service that you are working with will have no confidence in your ability as a worker in health and social care.

Deadlines

In any job, you will be given specific deadlines to complete particular tasks and working with adults is no different. For instance you may be asked to plan a leisure and creative activity for a group of adults with learning disabilities. If you fail to plan it in time, the group will be disappointed as they will miss out on their activity.

Check

- You need to be punctual when working with adults
- Sometimes you may have to work shifts
- Deadlines are important and help to keep a setting organised.

L02 Working as a team & problem solving

Discussing activities

Being a good team member means treating others with respect as this helps everyone work well together. When you are planning creative and leisure activities for adults, it is important to listen to other people's ideas. The adults who are using the service may have some ideas about what activities they would like to do as well as the people you work with.

Co-operation

When working with adults in health and social care settings, you must be supportive and help the other people in your team. You should ask politely whether they can help you do a particular task, or you can ask them if they need any help.

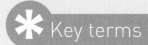

* Key terms

Co-operation
Working together to achieve a target or goal.

Solution
An answer to a problem.

! Remember

- Join in discussions and share ideas
- Ask for help when needed
- Look for ways to help others
- Follow instructions happily and without complaining.

Feedback

Receiving feedback is a key part of your development, and you should be ready to receive feedback to improve your own performance.

Feedback may come from your tutor, your placement supervisor or the adults that you are working with. The feedback you receive will most likely tell you what you did well, but it will also give you ideas of what you could do better in your next activity.

Feedback is important to our development

Problem solving

The difficulty with problem solving is that you often have to think of a solution to a problem rather quickly, as problems tend to occur when you are not expecting them.

A good way to deal with problems is to discuss them with your team and come up with solutions together. Sometimes you may have to think creatively to solve the problem. You may have to be flexible and carry out some activities or roles that you wouldn't usually do.

Case study:

Using your initiative

When carrying out creative and leisure activities, you are likely to encounter problems. How you deal with the problems you face will determine how successful your activity is.

Look at the problems below. With a partner, discuss ways in which you could avoid the problem and how you would deal with it.

1. **Lisa and Matthew are carrying out a creative activity. Matthew doesn't turn up and has all the materials and resources for the activity.**

2. **Shannon has planned a leisure activity for outdoors, but it is raining heavily.**

3. **Yuan has planned a creative activity for five people. Ten people say they would like to join in the activity.**

4. **Carmen notices that an adult working with David cannot understand David's Scottish accent.**

Functional skills

By taking part in a discussion, you will be demonstrating your English speaking and listening skills.

Check

- It is important to all work as a team
- Good team members support each other even when things go wrong
- To solve problems, you will need to co-operate and work as a team
- Solving problems may require you to think quickly.

L02 Health & safety

Personal safety and others

When you are carrying out a creative or leisure activity with adults, you must make sure that it is safe and appropriate for everyone. If the activity involves using dangerous tools and equipment, it may not be appropriate to do this activity with a particular group or with staff who are untrained in using the tools and equipment.

Safe use of tools

When you are planning your creative or leisure activity, you need to think about what tools your activity needs. Some tools may be unsafe for particular client groups, and the users of the service may need supervising or assisting while they are taking part in the activity.

Other tools may need to be adapted to suit the range and needs of the adults, for instance, adapting the grip on tools for people with arthritis.

Outdoor equipment

Adults using health and social care services often enjoy taking part in activities outdoors. The outdoor equipment that they use must be kept to a high standard of safety to make sure that it does not cause harm to anyone.

The equipment should be checked for damage before and after every use. If the equipment is mobile, then it should be stored indoors or under cover to ensure it stays in a good, safe condition.

! Remember

- Keep an eye on vulnerable adults when they are using sharp or dangerous equipment

- Make sure equipment is not damaged or broken before and after use

- Make sure you know how to use the equipment safely.

Always check your materials, tools and equipment before you use them

Risk assessment

When you plan a creative and leisure activity, such as going on an outing, you are usually expected to carry out a **risk assessment**. A risk assessment looks at how likely it is that someone will get hurt during the activity, whether any risks can be reduced and whether it is safe to carry out the activity.

Key term

Risk assessment
Looking at whether an activity could cause harm and deciding whether it is safe to continue.

Activity: Spot the health and safety hazards

You are observing some creative and leisure activities. What is wrong with the following?

1. A user of service is enjoying a cooking activity, but has a cut on their hand that is not covered by a plaster or disposable gloves.

2. A group of adults are taking part in an outdoor game of rounders, but the wooden bats are old and falling apart.

3. Paint bottles are stored next to drink bottles.

4. A group of people with learning disabilities are left to their sewing and knitting activities while the supervisor makes a cup of tea.

Check

- Activities should be safe for everyone

- Some groups of adults may need to be supervised when using tools

- Some activities and materials may need to be adapted to meet the needs of some adults

- A risk assessment should be completed when planning an activity.

L02 Application of number & application of IT

Maths awareness

When you are working in a health and social care setting, nobody will expect you to do long, complicated equations involving letters and numbers but you will need to understand basic **application of number**.

When you prepare an activity for adults, you must know how many adults are taking part in the activity, and how much equipment you need. This is an example of application of number as you are applying your understanding of numbers to a health and social care situation.

Being maths-aware helps in your planning of activities as you will need to consider how much time you need to set the activity up, how much time the activity will take, and how much time you need to clear up afterwards. You can then work out if you have enough time to carry out the activity in the timescale you have been given.

Applying maths to health and social care (in particular working with adults), makes you aware that maths occurs in almost everything we do, often when we do not realise it.

Key term

Application of number
Using numbers in a health and social care environment.

Case study:

Spot the maths

Jani is a work placement learner at a residential home. When asked about her course, Jani explains that she doesn't understand why she needs to learn application of number at school.

Jani tells her mother about her placement when she gets home. She describes to her mother what she has done that day.

1. **Looking over Jani's day, can you see any instances where Jani would have needed to apply her understanding of numbers and use any basic maths skills? If so, where?**

2. **What would you say to Jani if she told you she didn't understand why she needs to learn application of number?**

Basic IT skills

When working in a health and social care setting, you need to demonstrate **application of IT**. This means having some basic IT skills and being able to use a computer. Many people enjoy using social network sites and understand how to use search engines to surf the internet.

It is important to be safe when using the internet and to remember that you and others have a right to have your information kept confidential.

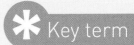 Key term

Application of IT
Using computers and information technology in a health and social care environment.

! Remember

- Have password protection on your computer
- Never share personal information about yourself or anyone you work with (including users of service) on networking sites (or anywhere)
- Bear in mind that not all websites are accurate.

Check

- Application of number and IT means using numbers and information technology in health and social care
- Maths and IT can be applied in any activity
- Information should be kept confidential.

L03 Communication skills & assessing own work

Literacy skills

Whether it be reading instructions on a board game to playing with a group of adults, or writing up the activities enjoyed by an individual, literacy is part of our day-to-day lives.

When working with adults, you may be asked to produce a record of the activities that you have carried out with them. This information will need to be organised and neatly presented, giving details of each activity.

Activity: Activity record

Produce a record of all the creative and leisure activities that you have completed with adults. You could put your record into a table style like the one below. Remember to make your record as detailed as possible and neatly presented.

Date	Start time	End time	Activity name	Creative or Leisure activity?	Client group	Number of people taking part in activity	Do the adults have any specific needs?	Description of activity and how it was run.	Tools, materials, resources, equipment needed	Problems encountered	Anything else?

Listening skills

Being a good communicator means that you are able to listen and ask questions effectively. Listening to others means thinking about what they are saying and then responding. You can respond appropriately by nodding your head, smiling and asking relevant questions.

Your placement supervisor or tutor may give you instructions or ask you to complete a task. It is very important that you listen carefully and ask questions if you do not understand, so you do not get the task wrong.

! Remember

- **Wait for the person to finish speaking before you speak**
- **Show you are listening**
- **Ask questions.**

Assessing your work

Your tutor or placement supervisor may ask you to think about what you are good at and what you need help with when it comes to doing creative and leisure activities with adults. They may provide you with some feedback as to how well you are getting on. Your tutor or placement supervisor might make some suggestions as to how you can improve and develop.

To check your progress and development, you could set some targets that help you to improve your performance and give you realistic goals to work towards.

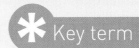
Key term

Scavenger hunt
A game where you have to find a number of items on a list.

Case study:
Elliot

Elliot has just completed his leisure activity with a group of adults who have a range of physical difficulties such as vision impairments, hearing impairments and mobility problems.

Elliot has planned a **scavenger hunt** as his activity. He has spent a lot of time researching the area where the hunt will take place and where all the items can be found. Elliot thinks that the scavenger hunt will be easy and that it will only take the group approximately 30 minutes. Two hours later, the group have not returned and Elliot has to find the adults and call an end to the activity.

Elliot is assessing his activity, but cannot work out why the hunt went on for so long. Can you help? What feedback would you give Elliot? Use the questions below as guidance.

1. Why do you think the hunt went on for so long?

2. What did Elliot do well?

3. What do you think Elliot needs to improve on?

Check

- Good communication skills give people confidence in your ability
- It is important to listen to instructions carefully
- Assessing your work helps you improve and develop your skills
- Tutors and placement supervisors can help you set targets.

ASSESSMENT OVERVIEW

While working through this unit, you will have prepared for completing the following assessment tasks:

○	1.1	Describe creative activities for adults	Pages 124–129
○	1.2	Describe leisure activities for adults	Pages 130–133
○	2.1	Participate in a creative and leisure activity for adults and demonstrate:	
		• self-management skills	Pages 134–135
		• a positive contribution as a team member	Pages 136–137
		• meeting agreed deadlines	Pages 134–135
		• problem-solving skills	Pages 136–137
		• safe practice	Pages 138–139
		• communication skills	Pages 142–143
		• the use of IT	Pages 140–141
○	3.1	Assess own work-related skills required for providing creative and leisure activities for adults	Pages 142–143

Assignment tips

- To help you pass this unit, you could produce a poster or similar with pictures and titles of a number of creative and leisure activities for adults.

- Make sure your activities are varied and that you have activities that are suitable for different adult groups with different needs.

- When carrying out an activity, make sure you take an active part and show what you can do.

- Make a checklist of what materials you need, who is responsible for what, and what time you need to be there.

- Remember to listen carefully to instructions and co-operate as a member of the team.

- Keep a diary or similar recording of all the activities you do and what your role is in each activity.

- Ask tutors or other helpers to sign your diary to confirm what you do in the activity.

- Ask them to comment on how well you do these jobs. Using these comments, make a list of areas where you need to do better and explain why.

PROMOTING HEALTHY EATING IN CARE

This unit will help you to develop the skills that you will need to prepare healthy drinks and snacks for groups of individuals in health and social care settings. You will find out about how the food that we eat can help to make us healthier, and how different types of food are more suitable for the different needs of individuals. You will have the chance to learn how to create and prepare healthy drinks and snacks.

In this unit you will:

- Find out how food helps to keep you healthy

- Learn about making drinks and snacks for all ages in health and social care settings

- Learn how to make particular healthy drinks and snacks for individuals' personal needs

How would you help provide a healthy diet to adults in your care?

L01 Choosing food for good health

Food is an important part of your physical and emotional health. To have good physical health, you need to eat a well-balanced diet and enjoy food from the five different **food groups** each day. Here is the eatwell plate which shows how much of what you eat should come from each food group.

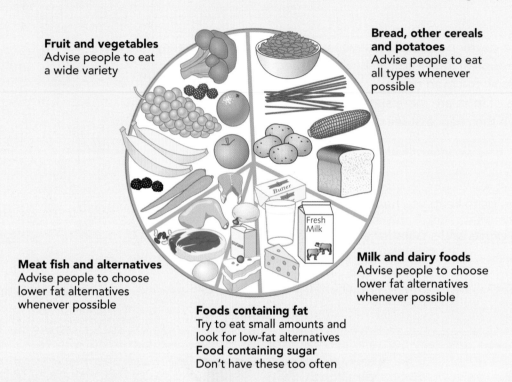

Fruit and vegetables
Advise people to eat a wide variety

Bread, other cereals and potatoes
Advise people to eat all types whenever possible

Meat fish and alternatives
Advise people to choose lower fat alternatives whenever possible

Foods containing fat
Try to eat small amounts and look for low-fat alternatives
Food containing sugar
Don't have these too often

Milk and dairy foods
Advise people to choose lower fat alternatives whenever possible

At each life stage you need different types and quantities of food. This means that you need different amounts of **vitamins** and **nutrients** at different times in your life.

◎ Activity: How much food do we need?

Find out how much of each of the following food groups babies, children and adults should eat. The NHS Live Well website is a good source of information.

1. Meat/fish and alternatives (beans and pulses)

2. Milk and dairy food

3. Fruit and vegetables

4. Food containing fat and sugar

5. Bread, cereals and potatoes.

Activity: Does my food look good enough to eat?

Working with a partner, make a poster showing three separate eatwell plates. There will be a plate for a small child, a plate for an adult and a plate for an older adult. Each plate should have the correct amounts of food for each food group and it should look colourful and appetising. You could collect photographs of food from magazines or from the internet.

Activity: How balanced is my diet?

You need to know that the food that you are preparing for the people in your care is **nutritionally balanced**. This quick test, using your own diet, will show whether you know how much of each of the food groups you should eat every day.

1. My diet needs to have .... portions of food like bread and pasta.

2. I need to have .... portions of fruit and vegetables a day.

3. I need to eat oily fish at least .... a week.

4. I need to avoid food that has .... in it.

5. I need to drink .... of water a day.

Write a paragraph explaining any changes to your diet that you think you should make.

Key term

Nutritionally balanced
Food that gives the correct balance of nutrients that the body needs.

Functional skills

By writing your paragraph, you will be demonstrating your English writing skills.

Check

- You need to eat a balanced diet to be healthy

- A balanced diet has the correct amount of all five food groups in it

- Individuals need different amounts of the five food groups at different life stages.

L01 Physical health

Preparing healthy food for different service users needs a lot of thought and attention. When you are preparing healthy food for people in your care, you need to think about their age and the balanced diet they need to ensure that they remain physically healthy. When you are an adult you need to eat a balanced diet without too much salt, sugar or fat. When you are over 65 you may need to eat fewer calories because you are less active or you may need smaller portions of food to make eating easier. Physical health includes the following.

Growth

Growth is the increase in size and mass that infants and children go through. It is important that infants and children get enough of the correct **nutrition** for them to grow up strong and healthy. For example, children need milk to develop strong bones. Children between four and 18 need lots of protein and **carbohydrates** because they are growing and using lots of energy.

Energy

Energy comes from the food we eat. It is measured in calories. Starchy foods like pasta contain a lot of calories, which provide energy and fuel for exercise.

Body function

Eating the right food allows our bodies to function properly. For example, vitamin C, which humans need for growth and repair, is found in fruits like oranges, lemons and grapefruit.

Repair

Food that helps our bodies to repair is easy to digest and high in protein, for example chicken. This is important to help adults recover after an operation.

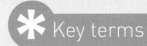

Key terms

Nutrition
The way that we take in and digest nutrients from food.

Carbohydrate
Foods such as pasta, rice, bread and potatoes that provide a lot of energy.

Children's food needs

This time line shows different key foods at different stages of a baby's development.

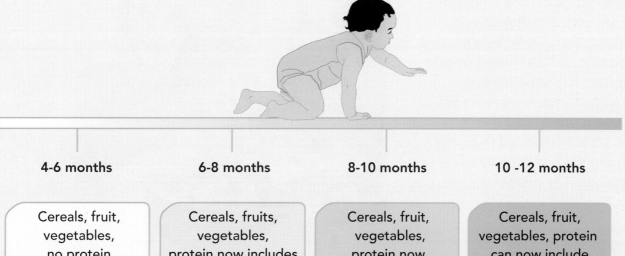

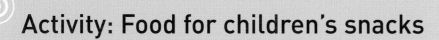

4-6 months	6-8 months	8-10 months	10-12 months
Cereals, fruit, vegetables, no protein or dairy	Cereals, fruits, vegetables, protein now includes small amounts of white meat	Cereals, fruit, vegetables, protein now includes eggs, beans and legumes, mild cheddars	Cereals, fruit, vegetables, protein can now include stronger cheeses, and dairy, now includes whole milk

Activity: Food for children's snacks

Food helps children to grow and develop. With a partner, choose six healthy snacks for a playgroup snack break. You will need to think about the **nutritional value** of the food, the ages of the children, their dietary needs and whether they can eat the food without help.

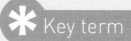 Key term

Nutritional value
The amount of nutrients provided by food.

Check

- You need different types of food at different life stages
- Children need carbohydrates for energy and growth.

L01 Emotional health

Sharing food and eating together helps to make it more enjoyable. Happy meals are relaxed and unhurried. Food is more attractive if it looks good and tastes good. Therefore, it is important to think about what food looks like and how it is presented on a table. Mealtimes need to give everyone the opportunity to be as independent as possible.

Why is it good to eat with others rather than eating your meal on your own in front of the television?

Activity: Are they enjoying their meal?

It is important to enjoy your food and the company you have when you are eating it.

Look at the people in the photo. Working with a partner, read through the list below and discuss why this meal will contribute to their emotional health.

- The food is balanced
- The food portion is easy to eat
- The people are happy.

Functional skills

Activity: Role-play

A good way to understand how people feel is to do a role-play. In groups, create a role-play about the characters in the photo. Each group should carry out the role-play and then you should all discuss your experiences and how they made you feel.

By having a discussion with your partner, you will be demonstrating your English speaking and listening skills.

Showing we care with food

The way that we prepare food for ourselves and for others can affect the way we feel about ourselves. If we take the time to find out the kinds of food people like and dislike, and prepare their food carefully, it means that we care about what we are doing and the person we are doing it for.

When we share food, we are enjoying each other's company as well. When we eat alone, we should prepare our food well because it means that we care about our own wellbeing.

Case study:

Arthur

Arthur has had to move into a care home because he has arthritis in his hands. This means that he has difficulty feeding himself because he cannot hold a knife and fork easily. He is not happy because he thinks that he will lose his independence in the care home.

Kamal is working with Arthur. He speaks to Arthur about the sorts of food that he likes, and when he prepares his food, he makes sure it does not require much cutting up.

1. **How will the steps above help Arthur to keep his independence?**

2. **How will these steps allow Arthur to enjoy eating with others?**

3. **Write a role-play imagining that you are introducing Arthur to other older adults in the care home. Think about how you would do it.**

✓ Check

- Being relaxed and unhurried when we eat helps us to digest and enjoy our food

- Finding out people's personal preferences, and taking care over the presentation of food is important

- We need to encourage independence at mealtimes for all age groups.

L02 Healthy drinks

Milk

A healthy drink can be a substitute for a meal if a person in your care cannot eat. Hot milk drinks can be very comforting and can help you to sleep. Milk is a good source of protein for all ages. However, it is especially important for older people as it can stop them developing brittle bones, and for young children as they need it for growth. Milk can be pasteurised or unpasteurised. Pregnant women are sometimes told not to drink **unpasteurised milk**.

Fresh fruit juice

Fresh fruit drinks and smoothies are a good source of vitamin C and can provide a balanced meal substitute when made with yogurt.

Water

You need to drink plenty of water every day to help your body to function properly. It is better to give children sugar-free drinks to protect their teeth.

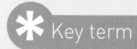

Key term

Unpasteurised milk
Milk that has not been treated to get rid of bacteria.

Activity: Know your drink

With some of your group, organise a trip to the local supermarket. Go to the fruit juice counter and buy a fresh fruit drink, a carton of long-life fruit juice and a bottle of squash of the same flavour. Take them back to your class and organise a tasting session. Put the drinks in different glasses, taste them and write down your answers to the following questions:

1. Which is the sweetest drink?

2. Which drink tastes most like the fruit that it is made from?

3. Can you tell the difference between the two types of fruit juice?

Now look at the ingredients on the containers

4. Which drink contains **preservatives**?

5. Which drink contains extra sugar?

Now decide which drink would be best for young children and which for vulnerable older adults. Why?

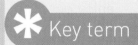

Key term

Preservatives
Chemicals that keep food eatable and drinkable for longer.

Why is orange juice a healthy drink for children?

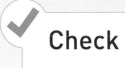

Check

- Some fruit drinks have lots of added sugar which means they are not good for you at any age

- You need to drink to stay healthy and to protect your kidneys.

L02 Healthy snacks

Fruit

The photo shows different types of fruit. Fresh fruit provides lots of vitamin C. However, dried fruit can be a good substitute as it is a portable snack that you can keep in your pocket to give you extra energy. This is important for all age groups.

Raw vegetables

Chopped up uncooked vegetables, such as carrots, cucumber, and courgettes, are delicious with dips.

How many fruit and vegetables can you identify in this image?

Wholemeal foods

Foods such as **wholemeal** cereals and brown bread, contain **fibre** which helps your digestion to work properly.

Eggs

Snacks made with eggs, such as scrambled egg on toast are very good if you have been ill as they can help your body to repair itself.

Choosing snacks from different food groups will ensure that you have a healthy and tasty mix of vitamins, carbohydrates and protein.

You need food to survive, but it is also important to enjoy your food. When you are planning a healthy snack, you need to think about the service user group that you are serving it to, and try to make sure that they will find it attractive as well as tasty. You also need to make sure that they can eat it. Don't give food that needs a lot of chewing to the old or the very young, for instance.

Nuts and seeds

Nuts and seeds are a very good source of protein. However, you should make sure that the person you are preparing them for is not allergic to them.

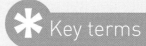
Key terms

Fibre
Parts of fruit, grains and vegetables that the body cannot digest, for instance bran.

Fibre helps the bowels to work properly.

Wholemeal
Foods made from brown flour, that is flour that contains bran, the hard skin of the wheat grain.

Activity: Is this the right food for your group?

You must think about how balanced your snack is. Here is a list of different healthy snacks. Write down whether they are suitable for babies, young children, adults or older adults.

- Fresh/dried/stewed fruit
- Raw vegetables and dips
- Yogurt
- Cereal with milk
- Cheese
- Bread as sandwiches, pitta bread and wraps
- Bread sticks.

Activity: Is this the right food for your group?

When you are catering for a group of children or adults, you need to design a menu. Choose a specific group and design a menu with five different snacks on it. They must be appropriate to your age group, balanced and tasty.

Now choose your favourite snack and either make it in school or at home. You could have a tasting session with others from your group.

Check

- Some foods are only suitable for particular age groups
- Menus need to be nutritionally balanced and designed for a specific age group.

L02 Groups in health & social care settings

It is easy to eat the wrong amounts of particular foods. This can cause problems even if the foods are from a healthy food group. Therefore, you need to know more about the needs of each individual that you prepare food for. If you are preparing food for young children, they will have different needs from teenagers, adults and older adults. The preparation and presentation of food can have an effect on whether the food is eaten by your clients and how much is eaten.

Young children

Activity: Preparing food for children in a nursery

Every morning children have a healthy food snack at nursery. They choose a snack and learn how to eat together.

Produce a small instruction leaflet that explains to a nursery assistant how to prepare food for children of different ages. You may find it useful to look back at your work from earlier in the unit to help you to design your snacks with the correct food balance.

Teenagers

Teenagers grow more slowly than younger children. However, they still need food that will help them develop. This means that they should eat food that provides protein, and energy-rich foods, such as pasta.

Older adults

As you get older, your food needs change. For example, you may be less active so you will need fewer calories; you may need more calcium for brittle bones; or you may need to have your food in smaller portions that can be chewed easily. However it is still important that you enjoy food and that you have a varied and interesting diet.

Functional skills

By producing your leaflet, you will be demonstrating your English writing skills.

Case study:

Arthur

We have already met Arthur who is a new resident in the care home. He wants to be independent, but has difficulty with food and therefore gets angry and frustrated at meal times. This means that he avoids eating with other people and asks for help. As a result he is also lonely and depressed.

You are told to care for Arthur and to help him to adjust to living in the home.

1. **In small groups, carry out some research about the appropriate food groups for an older adult and create a menu for Arthur. Make sure that you include hints about presentation.**

2. **Find out about different utensils that Arthur may use. This could involve writing to manufacturers and asking for samples that you can test. Or you could approach a local care home and ask if you could borrow some specialist eating equipment.**

Check

- We need to eat different types of food as we get older to help us to maintain our bodies

- Food should always look and taste appetising

- Food should be served using easy-to-use utensils that help to maintain a service user's independence.

L03 Hygiene & safety

Food storage

Food safety and hygiene are of vital importance in an area that deals with food preparation. However, they are especially important if you are working with people who may be vulnerable to infection.

! Remember

- Cover all food
- Chill cooked food quickly
- Make sure that you are storing food in the correct place in the fridge or freezer (For example, do not store raw meat above cooked meat)
- Eat food when it is fresh as food loses vitamins as it gets older
- Eat food before its use by date.

Hand washing

The most important food hygiene task that you can do is washing your hands frequently and always after you have been to the toilet.

! Remember

- Always wash your hands before preparing or serving food
- Use hot water and anti-bacterial soap or hand wash
- Use a clean towel or hot air blower to dry your hands (Remember if the towel is dirty you are putting bacteria straight back onto your hands)
- Avoid preparing food if you have a stomach bug
- Store food carefully at the right temperature.

How is this assistant ensuring that the area is free from bacteria?

Correct use of equipment

! Remember

- Make sure all utensils are clean

- Make sure that knives are sharp and stored safely

- Cut up meat and vegetables on separate chopping boards

- Check that you know how to use equipment such as knives and blenders safely.

Activity: Food safety in the preparation areas

Arrange with your tutor to visit your school canteen. Take the 'Remember' list above with you to check on the health and safety arrangements. Then carry out a check on your kitchen at home. Is it the same, better or worse?

Ensuring correct food is given to individuals

There are lots of different aspects of your life that can influence what you eat. These can be cultural beliefs, such as religion, which may mean that you do not want to eat beef or pork. Or you may be allergic to certain foods, or have a medical condition, such as diabetes, which would mean that you would have to be careful about the amount of sugar that you eat. It is important that you are aware of these preferences and needs when preparing food so that you keep people safe, happy and healthy.

Check

- You must always wash your hands before preparing food

- Food needs to be stored in the correct containers

- Food preparation areas must be safe and clean.

L03 Food presentation

Colour and arrangement

You see and smell food long before you taste it. How food looks and how it smells are important parts of the eating experience, especially if you are ill and have lost your appetite. You like food that has fresh colours and a variation of textures. Food should be placed with thought on the plate to show that you care.

Very young children need small amounts of food that has been **pureed** so that it can be easily swallowed and digested. The majority of their nourishment comes from drinking milk. As children get older they begin to like lumpier food with stronger tastes. They still need foods that will help to build strong teeth and bones.

As you grow, you develop more varied tastes. As you get older, you may find that certain foods gives you problems, such as **indigestion**, which can be painful.

Why does this presentation of food make it more appetizing?

Amount

You should also consider the size and consistency of each piece of food on the plate. People want to be independent when they eat, so it is important that the food you are preparing can be easily managed by whoever has to eat it. The person who is eating it may otherwise be embarrassed and unhappy.

Activity:
Have I presented the food correctly?

Imagine you are in charge of food preparation in either a nursery or a care home. Look for snack recipes on the internet and pictures to illustrate them. Find a range of recipes and pictures, showing both cooked and raw meals in both small and large portions.

Then match the pictures of the food to the type of individual who is most likely to enjoy it and write a sentence explaining why you have made this choice.

Display your findings on a poster.

Appropriate plates and bowls

When serving food to different individuals, you need to consider the plates and bowls that you are using. Choosing the correct dish will encourage people to eat their meals. Think about how big the plates are. Will a portion on a small plate look bigger than on a larger plate? Will the plates and bowls get in the way on the table? Will the patterns on the plates confuse people who are using them? How will people feel if the crockery is broken or chipped?

Think also about who will use your plates. A young child requires a small unbreakable bowl that will not topple over as this will encourage them to be independent. An older adult may need plates with similar properties.

Activity: Which bowl for which dish?

Use your poster to show an example of the type of dish that a child, teenager, adult and older adult may choose. Remember that they will all want to be independent when they eat.

Check

- Food should look and smell appetising
- Food should be nutritionally balanced
- Food portions need to be the correct size for the service user eating it.

L03 Health needs & individual needs

In health and social care, it is important that you look after people's particular health needs and that you respect people's different beliefs. Food can cause illness to become worse, or distress someone with particular food dislikes, so it is important to make sure that people in your care are not given food that could damage their health or wellbeing.

✳ Key term

Epipen
An instrument for giving medication for allergic reactions.

Diabetic health requirements

Good food contributes to your health, but in some cases particular food can make you ill.

If you are diabetic, your body cannot control the movement of glucose, a type of sugar, in your blood, this can make you very ill. If you have diabetes, you need to eat at regular intervals to control your blood sugar levels and be very careful about the types of food you eat, especially sugary and fatty foods.

Food allergies

Sometimes you can develop allergies to certain food types. One of the most common allergies is to peanuts. However, you can also be allergic or sensitive to wheat, eggs and dairy products.

Symptoms of food allergies can include a swollen mouth, tongue and throat, itchy eyes, a rash and an itchy mouth. Some of the symptoms can be severe and may need an **Epipen** to reduce them.

Coronary heart disease

Coronary heart disease can be made worse by eating saturated fats, such as animal fats, butter, cheese and full fat milk. If you do have this disease, you should eat food that is low in saturated fat.

People can use epipens on themselves

Personal preference and cultural needs

We often choose different foods because of personal preference or because of **cultural** and religious beliefs. For example, being vegetarian means that you do not eat meat and sometimes you may not eat dairy products. Muslims and Jews do not eat pork and Hindus believe that the cow is sacred so do not eat beef.

When you are caring for a person, it is important that you form a trusting relationship with them so that you understand the different preferences they may have and can help them to make their own choices.

Physical needs

If you are an active sports person, you need more high energy, starchy foods and proteins to give you energy and keep you fit. If you have a job sitting at a desk, you require less high energy food because you are less active. You need to know how many calories you require and which foods are low in unsaturated fat and therefore healthy.

Key term

Cultural
Relating to the way that we live.

Activity: Religious and cultural beliefs

Using books or the internet to help you research the word list below, complete these sentences about different beliefs. (You may have to use some of the words more than once.) Look up any words you do not understand.

1. Hindus are very strict ....
2. Muslims believe that meat and dairy products must be .... They will not eat ....
3. Sikhs are often .... and they will not eat ....
4. Jewish food must be .... they will not eat ....
5. Strict Catholics only eat .... on Wednesdays and Fridays.

Word list
vegetarians, fish, meat, kosher, halal, pork

Functional skills

Using the internet will help your IT skills.

Check

- Diabetics need to be very careful about their diet
- A food allergy can be very dangerous
- You must respect different cultural and religious beliefs about food.

ASSESSMENT OVERVIEW

While working through this unit, you will have prepared for completing the following assessment tasks:

○	1.1	Describe ways food contributes to the health of individuals	Pages 146–151
○	2.1	Outline healthy drinks and snacks for groups	Pages 152–157
○	3.1	Make healthy drinks and snacks to meet individual needs	Pages 158–159 162–163
○	3.2	Serve drinks and snacks to meet individual needs	Pages 160–161

edexcel

Assignment tips

- To help you pass this unit, you need to show that you understand the importance of serving food that is nutritionally balanced.

- Show in either a role-play or discussion that you understand how food can contribute to good emotional health.

- Show on a poster or leaflet that you have carried out research about healthy food.

- Design and make a healthy snack or drink for an individual service user.

- Show that you understand correct use of hygiene and how to serve food that is well presented and appetising.

- Provide evidence of all of your practical work.

COMMUNICATION WITH ADULTS & CHILDREN IN HEALTH & SOCIAL CARE

UNIT 18

Communication plays an important role in all workplaces, but even more so in places where people are being cared for. Having good communication skills will help build professional relationships with users of services, colleagues and other professionals. It will also help make the working environment much more pleasant to be in.

It is therefore important that you understand the ways in which different groups of people can communicate and how this information will help you to understand them.

This unit will introduce you to ways in which adults, children and babies communicate and will look at some barriers that may get in the way of these people communicating successfully.

In this unit you will:

- Learn about different forms of communication in health and social care settings

- Explore barriers to communication in health and social care settings

- Look at ways to communicate with adults with different needs in health and social care settings

- Discover ways to communicate with babies, children and young people in health and social care settings

How can you communicate with service users?

L01 Forms of communication

Communication is about interacting and sharing information with others. However, it is not just about the giving of information. Communication also involves listening to what others have to say and observing the non-verbal signals that people send during conversations.

One-to-one

A one-to-one conversation is a form of communication that is held between two individuals. It relies on body language to help put across messages and information.

Groups

There are many times when you will have conversations with more than one other person. These are known as group discussions. Group discussions need to be carried out in a way that encourages everyone to join in.

Formal

Formal communication takes place on an official basis. For example, it is the type of conversation that care staff would have to discuss a patient's care needs.

Informal

Informal communication takes place between people on a casual basis. For example, passing the time of day with someone that you do not know very well, or a chat with friends.

Verbal communication

Verbal communication is when information is passed to others with the use of spoken words.

Turn taking

When having a conversation, it is important that everyone has the opportunity to join in the discussion. This can be achieved by developing your skills in turn taking and not talking at the same time as others. If too many people try to talk at once, no one will hear what is being said and therefore no one will be able to listen.

Questioning

The use of questions when communicating with people is a very effective way of encouraging people to talk to you. It is also a good way of discovering information about people that they would not usually give to you freely.

A closed question only requires a person to answer with simple one word responses, like yes, no or maybe. To enable the conversation to flow, you will need to ask questions that encourage full responses. This will open up the conversation and help to avoid any awkward silences. This is called open questioning.

Key term

Active listening
Showing the person you are having a conversation with that you are interested in what they have to say.

Active listening

When you are talking to someone it is important that the person feels that you are interested in what they have to say. This is **active listening**.

Why is it important to look at the person who is talking in a discussion group?

Activity: Who can hear me?

You have probably taken part in group or class discussions at some point during your time at school or college. Can you think of an occasion during these discussions when you thought others were either talking at the same time as you, or not listening to what you had to say?

1. Explain how this made you feel.

2. What can you do to encourage people to listen to you?

3. Why is it important that people are given the opportunity to have their say?

Check

- There are several different forms of communication

- People can communicate verbally, through the use of words.

L01 More forms of communication

Non-verbal communication

Non-verbal communication is when information is passed to others without the use of spoken words. Examples of non-verbal communication include:

- *Body language*: body language plays a big role in the process of communication. Therefore, it is important that you understand what your body language is saying about you.

- *Facial expressions*: how your face looks when you are talking to someone, such as smiling or frowning.

- *Eye contact*: our eyes frequently give away what we are feeling. Avoiding eye contact with someone you are talking to can make them feel uncomfortable.

- *Posture*: this is the way in which people hold their body either standing or sitting. Sitting very upright with your arms folded can come across as though you are not interested. Lying back or slouching can look as though you are bored.

- *Use of hands*: some people use their hands to express themselves when they are talking. These hand movements are known as **gestures**. The use of gestures can be a good way of communicating with people when it is not possible to use spoken words. However, overuse of hand movements and gestures can be annoying and distract from the conversation.

- *Pauses*: these are the gaps that we leave during conversations. Pausing can tell the other person that you are waiting for them to respond, and it can also show that you are interested and listening.

What do you think this young girl could be describing?

 Key term

Gesture
An action or movement made with the body to communicate messages.

Written communication

Written communication is a form of non-verbal communication that is expressed through the use of words. There are many forms of written communication and it is important that care workers present written pieces of communication as clearly as possible. Written forms of communication have the advantage of being permanent and therefore can be looked at again if necessary.

Examples of written communication include:

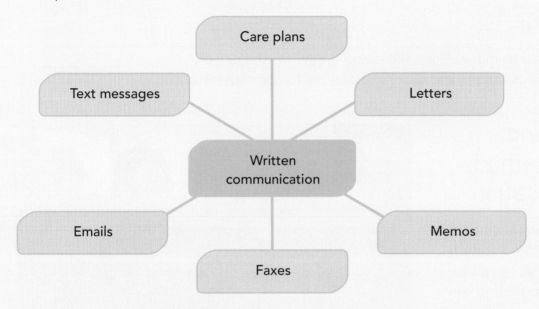

Activity: Ways to communicate in health and social care

Produce a leaflet that highlights four different forms of communication in health and social care settings.

Your leaflet should include clear descriptions on each form of communication. Don't forget to use colour and pictures to make your leaflet eye-catching.

Functional skills

By producing a leaflet, you will be demonstrating your English writing skills.

Check

- There are several different forms of communication
- Some forms of communication rely on the use of body language.

L01 Communicating with non-verbal children & adults

There will be times when you need to communicate with people who, because of their age, an illness or disability may have problems understanding you, or you understanding them.

Sign language

Sign language is used by many deaf people and it involves the use of hand shapes, hand movements and facial expressions to communicate.

Understanding individual methods of communication

Some people will have their own individual way of communicating with others and it is up to you to discover a person's preferred way of communicating.

Learning to sign from an early age

Importance of observing facial expression

During conversations it is important that you continually pay attention to the service user's facial expressions. This helps you to understand them further and discover any emotions that words sometimes cannot express.

People with learning disabilities and medical conditions may have to rely on the use of facial expressions to get their message across to you. The use of facial expressions may well be their only way of communicating their emotions, and they will trust you more freely if they feel you understand them.

Moods, reactions and gestures

There may be occasions when users of services are not in the mood for talking. This does not necessarily mean they are unhappy, it might simply mean that they don't feel like talking. Remember the reactions and gestures of people with medical conditions and disabilities may be different from those of other groups of people.

The need for patience

When you are talking to a person, it is important that you give them the time and opportunity to express themselves at their own pace. Rushing someone can make them frustrated and they may withdraw from the conversation. This can result in the breakdown of the patient-carer relationship, as the user of services may feel that you do not have time to listen to what they have to say.

Activity: I can't see you

Work in pairs with one person covering their eyes with a scarf.

1. Sit opposite each other and have a conversation. The conversation could be about anything that you want – maybe you could talk about what you did at the weekend or the last film or television programme you watched. Change roles after about five minutes.

2. How do you feel about not being able to see the other person when you are talking?

3. What can you do to help the conversation to feel more comfortable?

Check

- Some people can only communicate non-verbally
- Some people will have medical conditions that affect their non-verbal communication skills
- Having an awareness of non-verbal forms of communication will help you to communicate more effectively.

L01 Barriers to communication

There are various things that can cause communication not to happen as well as it could. These are called barriers to communication.

Physical barriers

A physical barrier to communication is something in the surroundings that stops a person from communicating effectively. For example, the place where the conversation is held may be noisy. This can result in the message not getting across correctly and the conversation may be confused.

Different language

Some people may not speak English as their first language and therefore you may have difficulty understanding each other.

Impairments

Some people will have impairments that can stop them from communicating effectively, for instance, they are unable to see, hear or talk as well as they should.

Emotional factors

Emotional factors can affect the way in which a person communicates. Examples of these factors include:

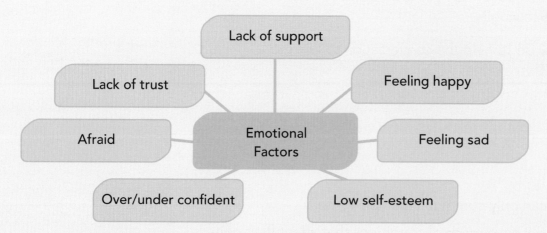

Complex language

When communicating with others, it is important to speak to them in words they can understand. If you use complicated words, some people may feel confused and find it difficult to understand you.

Use of jargon

Jargon is when people use technical words throughout a conversation. The use of jargon can be confusing for some and they may withdraw from the conversation.

Patronising communication

It is important that you communicate with users of services and their families in a non-**patronising** way. You must speak to people respectfully and call them by their preferred name. You need to use words that the person will be able to understand and in a tone that is suitable for the conversation.

Cultural differences

It is important to remember that some people's cultures will be different from your own. However, you should not make assumptions about a particular group of people. Assumptions can lead to labelling and stereotyping, which can result in confusion and misunderstanding.

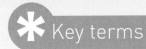

Key terms

Jargon
Language and words only used by particular groups.

Patronising
Treating someone as if they were not as clever as you.

Activity: Am I patronising?

Edward and Kathryn are both carers at St Mark's care home. Edward always makes a point of talking to the service users and finds out what name they would like to be called by. However, Kathryn does not do this and calls everyone 'dearie' or 'love'.

1. Who do you think is right?

2. Give reasons for your choice.

3. How should carers address users of services?

4. Explain how addressing users of services in the way they prefer will help with patient and carer relationships.

✓ Check

- There are various different barriers to communication
- Communication barriers stop people from joining in and make them feel isolated
- Being aware of different barriers to communication will help you to find alternative ways of communicating.

L02 Communicating with different groups of adults

You are one of a kind and there is no one exactly the same as you. However, some people may be similar to you in their values and beliefs. This is because of your culture and the influence it has on the social groups that you belong to. There may also be groups that you belong to because of your shared circumstances.

Senior citizens

Senior citizens have lived for a long time and usually don't like people being over-familiar with them. They also like to be called by a name of their own choice. Assumptions are quite often made about senior citizens and it is tempting to speak to them in a much louder voice than you normally would. Quite often people assume that because they are old, they are no longer able to make decisions or do things for themselves. Here are some important points when caring for senior citizens:

It is important to some senior citizens to remain independent

! Remember

Remember to:

- Ask them their name
- Ask what help they need
- Be respectful
- Be aware of any health issues they may have
- Speak clearly
- Be patient
- Don't talk over them
- Smile and be friendly.

People with disabilities

You need to communicate with people with disabilities in a manner that best suits their needs.

Disability	Definition	How to communicate
Sensory	Senses, such as sight or hearing are not as good as they should be	Ask what help they need: hearing aids, eye glasses, large-print books. Talk slower, be patient, use sign language
Learning	Unable to understand or remember information as well as they should	Take time talking to them, check they have understood, write things down
Emotional	Easily upset or annoyed	Give them time, be patient, talk about things of their own choice
Physical	Something to do with the body	Be aware of their disability, give them choices

People affected by illness or frailty

There will be times when people may be too frail or ill to communicate effectively. Support from family or friends may help to ensure that information has been understood.

Case study:

Edwin and Mark

Edwin is 84 and has recently moved to the local residential care home. His son, Mark, decides it is for the best because he has **Parkinson's disease** and is also becoming increasingly forgetful. Edwin does not want to move to the home, but is afraid to refuse in case his son gets cross with him. However, on a recent visit his son notices that Edwin is becoming withdrawn and appears confused and upset.

1. **How do you think Mark deals with the situation before Edwin goes in to the home?**

2. **What can Mark do now?**

Key term

Parkinson's Disease
A disorder of the nervous system that makes people weak and affects mobility.

Check

- There are several different groups of adults that you will have to communicate with

- Care workers must be aware of the different adult groups to communicate with them effectively

- You must understand how to communicate with each group of adults.

L02 Ways to communicate with adults

There are various different ways in which you can communicate with adults in health and social care settings. It is important that you find out as much as possible about your client's communication skills prior to discussing anything with them.

Show respect

Adults should be treated in a respectful manner. You can show respect by:

- Listening to them
- Not interrupting them
- Giving them time
- Being polite
- Not being patronising.

Appropriate body language

When talking to adult service users it is important that you are aware of the non-verbal messages and signals that your body may be giving out. Here are some important tips:

- Do not stand too close to the service user (do not invade their personal space)
- Stand or sit straight
- Look interested in what the person has to say by nodding your head at appropriate times.

Undivided attention

There is nothing more annoying than trying to have a conversation with someone and it is interrupted by something. You must avoid interruptions as much as possible, for instance by turning off your mobile phone, as this will make users of services feel that you are interested in what they have to say and you are giving them your undivided attention.

How is this doctor using appropriate body language?

Calm listening

During conversations you must listen in a calm manner and talk in a quiet, steady voice. You need to be aware of the signals and messages that your body language and facial expressions may give out.

Give time for responses

You must give users of services enough time to respond to you. Rushing or hurrying them may result in them responding in a way that they do not really mean.

Check understanding

Sometimes people do not understand or misunderstand what is being said. Therefore, it is important that you check the person understands the information you are giving them. You can do this by asking the person to repeat back to you in their own words what you have told them.

Case study:

What about me?

Andrew is the manager of the local care home. He has arranged an appointment with one of the residents in his care to discuss the funding of their care. Just as they are about to start the conversation the telephone rings. Andrew answers it and spends about five minutes chatting to the caller. After he has finished, he continues the conversation with the resident. However, as he is doing so, he is reading the case notes of another person in the home.

1. What is Andrew doing wrong?

2. How do you think the resident might be feeling?

3. Explain, with examples, what Andrew should do differently.

Check

- Adults communicate in many different ways
- You should be aware of a person's body language
- It is important that you pay attention to the person you are talking to.

L02 More ways to communicate with adults

Avoid being patronising

When communicating with adults, it is important not to treat them as though they were less intelligent than you. You should talk to them on an equal level.

Use of signs

Signs can be used to help adults who have lost their hearing to understand what is going on. Signs can be made with:

- Arms

- Hands

- Symbols

- Diagrams

- Pictures.

Pictures

Using pictures with people that have communication problems can be very helpful. Images can help a person to understand and join in a conversation, when they might otherwise feel **isolated**.

Lip reading

Some people are unable to hear as well as they should, and they use the skill of reading people's lips when they are talking to communicate. They look at the lips and facial expressions that someone is making, and use these to interpret what they are saying.

Translator

A translator is a person who works as a go-between to translate one language to another. This ensures that people who do not understand the language being used can join in and do not feel isolated.

The alphabet in British Sign Language. Do you know any of these signs?

* Key term

Isolated
Feeling alone and with no family, friends or support.

Eye contact

When having a conversation it is essential that you use positive eye contact. This means you should:

- Look at the person you are talking to
- Not stare
- Be aware of cultural differences (some cultures avoid direct eye contact to show respect).

Awareness of cultural differences

The UK is an increasingly **multicultural** country and people from many different cultures, ethnicity, race and backgrounds live here.

Communicating with people whose culture is different from your own can be challenging. However, it is essential that you interact in a way that shows you value and respect the person that you are talking to. Here are some examples of how this can be done:

- Don't make assumptions
- Avoid stereotyping
- Check understanding
- Be aware of non-verbal messages that you may be giving

Key term

Multicultural
Different groups of people from different countries, ethnic groups or religions living in the same society.

Activity: Without words?

Use magazines and internet images to make a comic strip that tells a story about something you are interested in. Your story can be about anything you like; however you must not include any written words within it. Don't forget to use colours to help convey information and make your comic strip more interesting.

Once completed, give your comic strip to another learner and ask them the following:

1. What is your story about?
2. What is good about your comic strip?
3. How could you make your comic strip better?

Check

- You should find out a person's preferred method of communicating
- Find alternative ways to communicate with people
- You must be aware of cultural differences.

L03 Communicating with babies, children & young people

It is very important to communicate effectively with young people, children and babies. This section will help you to understand how this can be done in health and social care.

Babies

Babies learn to communicate with their main carers very quickly. They cry to let you know that there is something wrong. For example, if they are tired, hungry, cold or need a clean nappy.

Babies also make lots of other noises that show how they are feeling. For example, cooing, babbling, screeching and gurgling.

Children

Children usually speak in simple sentences, using long words or complicated sentences will confuse them. It is essential that you use words that they understand. However, children are constantly learning and their **vocabulary** is continually growing, so it is also important that you encourage them to develop their language skills.

* Key term

Vocabulary
Set of words.

Teenagers

By the time a person reaches their teens, they will have built up a much larger vocabulary of words that they use and understand. However, they may still feel a little wary of carers and you will have to adapt your conversation to suit their individual needs.

Teenagers expect to be spoken to honestly and clearly, without being patronised. You should keep your personal opinions on their likes and dislikes to yourself, otherwise they may think that you don't like them and this could spoil the professional relationship that you have with them.

How can images be used to improve communication?

Children with disabilities

Children with disabilities may need help or support in communicating effectively. For children with sight difficulties, this can be in the form of visual aids such as:

- Signs
- Pictures
- Eye glasses
- Written information
- **Braille**
- Large-print books.

Children with hearing difficulties can be helped by:

- Using hearing aids
- Sitting closer to the speaker
- Learning to use sign language or to lip read.

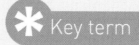

Key term

Braille
A form of writing for people with visual impairment that consists of raised dots and patterns that a person can read by touch.

Those affected by illness or frailty

Some children are unfortunate to have illnesses that cause them to be frailer than most children. This might mean they tire easily and struggle to hold conversations for long periods of time. It is vital that you take into account the child's condition and allow them to decide how the conversation should be led.

Activity: Forms of communication

List as many forms of communication for the following groups as you can:

- Babies
- Children
- Teenagers
- Those with disabilities
- Those who are frail or ill.

Check

- There are several different groups of young people
- Each group has its own preferred style of communicating, depending on its level and needs
- Children and young people have a right to be listened to.

L03 Ways to communicate with babies, children & young people

When you are having conversations with children, you must be aware of suitable ways to communicate with them effectively.

Using language appropriate to stage of development

The level of the language that you choose to use when talking to children will depend on the developmental stage of the children you are talking to. You should use words suitable for that stage.

Communicating at the same level and establishing bond/rapport

Sitting at the same level as children, listening and making time for them can help to establish a **rapport** with them.

Avoiding patronising communication and give time

Communication can be confused or misunderstood if not enough time is given for the conversation to happen properly. Remember to avoid patronising children, do not dismiss things that they have to say and respect their opinion.

Active listening

Active listening involves:

- Showing you are interested
- Hearing what has been said
- Remembering the conversation
- Checking for understanding.

Checking understanding

You can check someone has understood by:

- Asking questions
- Getting them to repeat the conversation back
- Observing body language
- Watching eyes and facial expressions.

✱ Key term

Rapport
An unspoken understanding between people.

How can this tutor check the child is understanding the task?

Open questions

When having a conversation, you need to use open-ended questions for the conversation to flow. This means asking questions in a way that ensures the child has to give you full answers rather than a simple yes, no, or maybe.

Being a good role model

Being a good role model means setting a good example to others around you. Children are constantly learning and they will pick up on things that you say or do. It is important that you:

- Use appropriate language
- Show respect.
- Don't swear

Using signs, pictures and translators

Signs and pictures are visual and some children can remember signs much quicker than words. Translators are used to help children whose language is different from yours to understand what is going on.

Activity: Hand washing poster

Raj is the manager of the local nursery. He has noticed that some of the children are reluctant to wash their hands when they are told to do so. Raj has decided that he will put some posters up around the nursery. He wants them to show the children when and how to wash their hands, and has asked for your help in doing this.

Make a poster that is suitable to put on a nursery wall. Remember your poster must:

- Be appropriate for the level of the children
- Show the children when to wash their hands
- Show them how to wash their hands.

Functional skills

By making a poster, you will be demonstrating your English writing skills.

Check

- Children and young people communicate in several different ways
- Effective communication helps to build positive relationships
- It is your responsibility to be a good role model.

ASSESSMENT OVERVIEW

While working through this unit, you will have prepared for completing the following assessment tasks:

◯	1.1 Outline different forms of communication	Pages 166–169
◯	1.2 Describe barriers to communication in health and social care	Pages 170–173
◯	2.1 Explain ways to communicate with adults with different needs in health and social care	Pages 174–179
◯	3.1 Explain ways to communicate with babies, children and young people in health and social care	Pages 180–183

edexcel

Assignment tips

- To help you pass this unit, you could produce a booklet that outlines different forms of communication in health and social care settings. The booklet should include barriers to the forms of communication you have outlined, and ways in which the barriers can be reduced or removed.

- Complete a worksheet that explains how to communicate with adults with different needs, or give a description of how staff communicated with adults with different needs at your work placement.

- Produce some case studies which illustrate how to communicate with babies, children and young people.

- Alternatively, write a report that explains how you have communicated with babies, young people and children at your work placement.

JOB OPPORTUNITIES IN HEALTH & SOCIAL CARE

This unit is about your choices and your future. You have chosen to study health and social care because you care about people and you are interested in helping them. This unit will help you to plan for you career in health and social care by looking at different job opportunities, the qualifications that each job needs and the skills and qualities that you will need to do them well.

In this unit you will:

- Learn about different job opportunities in health and social care
- Learn about the different qualifications and skills that you will need
- Learn about the hours you will work and the pay you will receive
- Plan for your first job interview

How many different job roles in health and social care can you think of?

L01 Job opportunities in the health care sector

There are two main job types in the health care **sector**. They are:

- Jobs that work with service users (**direct care worker**)

- Jobs that support people who are working with the service users (**indirect care worker**).

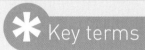

Key terms

Sector
A distinct part of the national health and social care system that care workers are employed in.

Direct care worker
Someone who works with service users.

Indirect care worker
Someone who supports people who are working with service users.

Immunisation
Giving of substances called vaccines, usually by injection, that help prevent disease.

Activity: Direct or indirect care?

Read this list of jobs and then divide them into direct care jobs and indirect care jobs.

Health care assistant, receptionist, adult's nurse, cleaners, children's nurse, doctor's secretary, learning disabilities nurse, midwife, dental nurse, ambulance care assistant, paramedic, emergency call handler, mental health nurse, hospital porter.

Direct care workers

Case study:

Health care visitor

Mary is a health care visitor. She visits families with children under five. She provides support and advice to parents to make sure that children are healthy and growing normally. Part of her job is to identify problems like asthma so that they can be treated. She also gives advice about **immunisations**, teething and behaviour.

1. **Would you want to do this job? Give reasons for your answer.**

Indirect care workers

Case study:

Receptionist

Lauren is a receptionist at a busy health centre. Her job is important to the day-to-day management of any health-care provision service. She organises appointments, manages files, makes sure that all patient records are kept securely, directs patients and carries out all clerical activities that are required by the practice.

1. What do you think is a receptionist's most important skill?

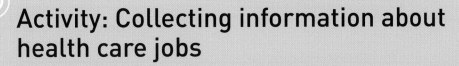

Activity: Collecting information about health care jobs

Choose two other direct care jobs and two indirect care jobs that you find interesting and answer the questions below:

1. What is the job title?

2. What are the main points from the job description?

3. Why are you interested in this job?

Your tutor will help you to find this information. For example, the NHS website is a useful source of information about health care jobs.

The local newspapers or TV soaps are also good places to find information as they will give you some ideas about the type of work involved in the job you are looking at.

Check

- There are direct care health workers and indirect care health workers

- You can work with any age group in the health care sector

- It is important that you have good people skills to work in the health care sector.

187

L01 Job opportunities in the social care sector

Jobs in the social care sector can be either community-based or residential-based. The aim of all social care sector jobs is to improve the lives, health and wellbeing of children, young people and adults. If you choose a job in this area, you will have a full and rewarding life.

Jobs in the social care sector include:

Community work

Community workers work with service users in the local area.

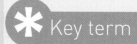

Case study:

Community worker with families

Asha has just got a job with Sure Start. It involves providing anti-natal advice, parenting skills advice, working with babies and toddlers, helping families to access good affordable childcare and helping families in difficulty. Principally, Sure Start helps families to stay together and be happy as a family group. Asha will have to be sensitive to the families' needs, be supportive and give advice without becoming involved in a personal way.

1. **In groups, discuss how Asha could use the following methods to be supportive to a family in difficulty:**

   - Listening
   - Providing advice
   - Going with them to see a professional adviser
   - Providing respite care
   - Providing care for children.

2. **Which do you think is the best method that can be used? Why?**

✳ Key term

Community worker
Someone who works with all service users in the local area.

Residential work

A **residential worker** is a person who works with service users in a home environment. This may be with older adults or young people. Examples of support for a service user in residential care include:

- Taking them food shopping
- Helping them to use public transport
- Helping them to give up drugs or alcohol.

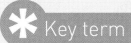

Key term

Residential worker
Someone who works in care homes (for older adults or young people).

Case study:
Residential care worker with adults

Stuart works as a residential care worker. His job can involve supporting a wide range of service users and building trusting relationships between them and their support workers. He supports clients with physical or learning disabilities, mental health conditions and drug or alcohol dependency. Stuart may also be involved in providing physical care, offering individual counselling, leading group therapy sessions or teaching.

1. Why is it important to encourage people in care to learn to be independent?

Activity: Finding out more about social care work

Carry out research on job roles in community and residential care work. Looking at each job role, answer the following questions:

1. What is the job title?
2. What are the main points from the job description?
3. Why are you interested in this job?

The Connexions website is a useful source of information.

✓ Check

- Social care workers can work in the community or in residential care
- They work with all age groups
- They help people to be independent and cope with day-to-day living.

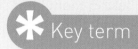

L01 Job opportunities in children's services

Children's services exist so that children and young people will have the best possible start in life. The Children and Young People's Service provides a wide range of services, so there are many interesting job opportunities. Here are some examples:

✱ Key term

Children's services
A sector of health and social care provision that focuses on the care of children.

Job Title	Job Description
Portage worker	Provides specialist nursery support for a child who is not in mainstream school to bring them to an appropriate level to join mainstream schooling
Early year's practitioner	Works with very young children
Childminder	Looks after children in the childminder's own home while their parents are at work
Play worker	A volunteer who works in a play group
Crèche worker	Looks after young children between six weeks and three years in a crèche
Early years teacher	Teaches young children in the first years of primary school
Hospital play specialist	Helps young children in hospital to recover through play

Case study:

Nursery assistant

A nursery assistant must be trustworthy and responsible. A nursery assistant may care for any child under the age of eight. They can work in a wide range of settings, such as schools, crèches, hospitals and residential homes. A very specialist type of nursery worker is a portage worker who works with children in their own homes to provide activities and routines that will help them to develop to the same levels of ability as other children by the time they reach school age.

1. **Research what a portage worker does to help to make a child more confident?**

2. **Research why is it important for a parent to feel that a nursery assistant is completely trustworthy?**

Activity: Finding out more about jobs in children's services

Write a short summary of two more jobs in children's services. You need to include the following information:

1. What is the job title?

2. What are the main points from the job description?

3. What specific areas of the job are you interested in?

Your tutor will help you to find this information. The Connexions website is a useful source of information.

 Functional skills

By writing your summary, you will be demonstrating your English writing skills.

Job shadowing

The best way to investigate a job you are really interested in is by carrying out a job shadowing day. This will tell you if the job is really right for you. When you arrange your job shadowing, there are important things you need to do:

! Remember

Remember to:

- Ask for advice from your Connexions adviser. The research that you have already carried out will help you talk about why you are interested in the job area that you have chosen.

- Write a letter of introduction to the person that you are hoping to shadow.

- Apply for a CRB check, if required for the area you are interested in. (See page 195 for more information about CRB checks.)

- Ask someone to write a reference for you.

- Come up with a list of questions to ask the person that you are shadowing.

 ## Check

- Job shadowing provides first-hand experience of a job role

- All work with vulnerable people needs a CRB check

- All jobs require a reference.

L02 Work patterns, pay & benefits

A new job can mean that you will need to make changes to your life. You must know the hours that you have to work and when you have to carry them out (**work pattern**). You will also need to know how much you are going to get paid, whether you have holiday pay and what the **benefits** are, for example, will you have a pension?

Work patterns

The way that we work can have a big effect on our lives and the lives of our families. Very few people have the traditional 9am till 5pm job that used to exist. Instead, we work a fixed number of hours in a week that can be broken up into different work patterns. They can be:

- *Shift work:* working a portion of the day. This can be as short as two hours or as long as eight hours, and can vary from week to week. It can also include early starts, late finishes and working at night or at weekends.

- *Irregular work patterns:* working when you are needed, not on a fixed pattern

- *Flexitime:* choosing when you work around a core fixed time per day

- *Annual leave:* the amount of holiday that you are allowed. This is a fixed amount of time that is worked out as a proportion of the amount of time that you work.

✳ Key terms

Work pattern
The hours that you have to work and when you have to carry them out.

Benefits
Rewards given to employees in addition to their salary.

Why do some jobs can require an early start?

Pay in health and social care jobs

When you start a new job or you are trying to find out about a career, you will need to make sure that you understand about how you will be paid and how your pay should improve. You may be paid weekly or monthly. You should find out about the **salary scale** for your job, and what the **pay increments** over time will be.

Benefits

Benefits are really important in any job as they make you feel valued. It is good to feel that you are getting better at what you do, and a pay increment can show how much you have improved. It is also important to feel that you have something to look forward to in the future when you have finished working and a good pension will give you that.

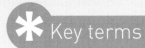

Key terms

Salary scale
The pay range for a particular type of work.

Pay increments
How much your pay will improve over time.

Subsidised
When part of the cost of something is paid by your employer.

Activity: Benefits for the future

What are the advantages and disadvantages of the following benefits? Remember you need to look to the future to see the full gain of most benefits.

1. Pension
2. Bonus for overtime
3. Uniform or clothing allowance
4. **Subsidised** or free meals
5. Training or professional development.

Check

- There are many different ways that working hours can be spread through the week

- You can be paid in a number of different ways, for instance weekly or monthly

- Benefits can be payments for overtime, uniforms or free meals, or they can be long-term, such as a pension

- Extra training is also a benefit because it will help you to develop your career.

L03 Qualifications & requirements

Qualifications

Qualifications are important and it is never too late to start studying. Qualifications are really useful to an employer because they tell them what you can do. They are either *essential* which means you *must* hold the qualification to get the job, or they are *desirable* which means the employer would like to see these, but may be prepared to employ you without holding the qualification before you start. They may ask you to study for this once you start work.

The different types of qualifications you may require to work in health and social care are:

Qualification	Definition	Examples
General	These are qualifications in particular academic subjects.	GCSEs, GCEs
Work-based	These are jobs that provide you with skills to use in the workplace.	Diplomas
Vocational	These qualifications are in specific work-related areas.	BTEC Firsts, Nationals, Apprenticeships
Practical	These are certificates that show that you have had training in a specific area.	Food handling, moving and lifting, first aid
Higher	These qualifications provide a more advanced education in a specific area.	Degree

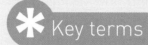
Key terms

Qualification
Gained when you successfully complete a course by passing an exam. For example, a BTEC is a vocational qualification, a GCSE is a general qualification.

Vocational (qualification)
Qualification that teaches you skills that will help you to do a job.

Practical (qualification)
Certificate that gives you day-to-day support and help with needs.

Criminal Records Bureau check

The Criminal Records Bureau (CRB) check consists of a single document that is used by all workplaces in health and social care sectors. It provides information about any criminal records that an employee may have. The CRB check agrees with an organisation's code of practice.

Other qualities

You must remember that qualifications are not the only important thing that an employer will need to know. Being caring and considerate are also a key part of who you are and how well suited you are to a job in this sector.

An example of a CRB form

Activity: Learning how to read job advertisements

Use a situations vacant column from a health and social care magazine for this activity. Read through several job descriptions and decide whether vocational, work-related or general qualifications would be best to help you to get these jobs and why.

Check

- A qualification tells an employer about knowledge that you have from studying

- A CRB check is important because it tells an employer that you are trustworthy.

L03 Skills & qualities

A skill is something that can be learnt, whereas a **quality** is something that you are born with. Different jobs require different types of skills and qualities.

Personal qualities

Health and social care requires you to be able to fully understand the position of those you are caring for. You must be caring, empathetic, gentle, and respectful.

Work-related skills

This area involves considerable people skills, such as being a good team member who communicates well. You will need to be able to think through problems and be well organised.

Level of fitness

You will be caring for people who will be relying on you, so it is important to look after your own health so that you do not let them down.

✳ Key term

Quality
A personal way of behaving that you do well.

Case study:

Julie, the nursery worker

Julie has been a nursery worker for ten years. The children love her because she is kind but firm and they feel safe with her. She enjoys her job because there are never two days the same and she likes dealing with the challenges, meeting new people and working with the rest of the team.

1. **Explain how Julie makes the children feel safe by being kind but firm.**

2. **Describe two different challenges that Julie might have to deal with as part of her job.**

Activity: What skills and qualities do I need?

Using the table below, list the different types of skills and qualities that are needed for a job in the health sector, a job in the social care sector and a job in children's services.

Sector	Job title	Skill	Quality
Health sector		1. 2.	1. 2.
Social care sector		1. 2.	1. 2.
Children's services		1. 2.	1. 2.

Check

- A skill is something you do well, and a quality is a personal way of behaving well.

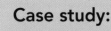
L03 Qualifications & skills: Case studies

When you are starting a new job or choosing a career, you need to think about the **terms and conditions** of employment, and the qualifications that you will need to do the job. A job is not just about qualifications and money; it is about making a difference and caring about other people. The best way to consider all of these points is to look at how they might affect another person. Read through these case studies and think about what advice you would give.

✻ Key term

Terms and conditions
The hours that you have to work, your pay and how many days' holiday you get.

Case study:

Annie

Annie has two children, Coral who is 15, and Alfie who is five. Annie decides that she wants to train as a health care assistant. She sees an advert for this role at her local GP's surgery and she feels that the job is just right for her. The job is 35 hours per week and pays £20,000 a year. However, she will have to study for a health and social care qualification and the job will involve a lot of responsibility. She will need to travel to patients in their homes to measure their blood pressure, glucose levels or change dressings.

1. **Will Annie be able to fit both work and her family into her life?**

2. **Why is it important to Annie to have a career?**

3. **How long will it take Annie to get her qualification?**

4. **Will Annie be able to take time off if she needs to?**

5. **List three skills and three qualities that she will need to work well in this area.**

Case study:

John

John has lived alone since his divorce. He has worked for a number of years in a bank (he is a qualified financial adviser) and has now decided that he would like a job where he can make a difference and meet new people. He feels that he can offer support to people who may be going through a difficult period in their lives. He has heard about the youth offending team through a friend who is a policeman. This kind of work appeals to John as working with young people would make him feel valued.

1. **Do you think John would be a good candidate for this job?**

2. **Why is it important that John can be flexible in this job?**

3. **How will this job give John a new approach to his life?**

4. **What are the qualifications and training that he will need for this job?**

5. **What skills and qualities will he require?**

Activity: The job I want

Design an A4 leaflet for a potential job applicant for the job that you shadowed for the day. It is important to describe the personal benefits of working in health and social care, as well as to explain the terms and conditions of the job.

Functional skills

By making your leaflet, you will be demonstrating your **English** writing skills.

Check

- A job may require you to get extra qualifications

- When you are looking for a job, it is important to know what area you want to work in.

- You should read adverts carefully and make sure that you can fulfil all of the job description.

L04 Career planning

It is crunch time, you have worked hard to get your qualifications and now you need to get a job. The most important thing to remember is that you may be working in this area for a substantial period of your life, so you need to make the right choices now.

Who are you?

Everyone finds it difficult to describe themselves, so a good starting point is to carry out a **personal skills audit**. To do this well, you need a partner to interview (not your best friend who may not feel they can tell you the truth). They will also interview you. The best way to carry out an interview is to find a quiet room to use. It is important that you are not disturbed. You need to have a list of questions to ask. The next activity will help you.

Key term

Personal skills audit
Looking realistically at the skills that you have and whether these are the ones that you will need to do a job well.

Activity: Planning an interview

Your interview needs careful planning. Make sure you know the skills and qualities needed for the job, so that you can ask your partner clear questions about how well they can do the job.

When writing questions for the interview, think about:

1. *Abilities* – The things you are good at

2. *Skills* – The things you can do

3. *Lifestyle* – The way that you live your life

4. *Values* – The aspects of your life that you consider important and would not change

5. *Personal qualities* – The unique aspects of your personality that define you

6. *Interests and hobbies* – Special activities that are personal to you

7. *Constraints* – Things that might stop you from doing the job. For example, if you are selected for the job, can you get there? Will shift working affect you or your family? Do you have the correct qualifications?

Functional skills

By carrying out an interview, you will be demonstrating your **English** speaking and listening skills.

Interviewing helps people to find out about each other

Check

- When you are looking for your first job, you should know what you would like to do, but you should also be flexible about the jobs that you are offered

- You need a personal reference that will tell your future employer about you

- You need to have the skills and qualities given in the job description.

L04 Finding out about jobs

Finding a job can be difficult so it is important that you have a plan, that you decide what you want to do and how far you can travel to do it. Keep an eye on your local newspaper for advertisements. Connexions are also helpful. They give advice to young people about careers and courses. You could also go to a careers fair. Many schools, trainers and city councils organise these on a regular basis. Local employers have displays and offer advice to people who want to work for them.

* Key term

Pathway
The possible direction that your career could take in the future.

Ask your centre if they have a Connexions office

◎ Activity: Working together for the future

In your groups, investigate three different job areas (**pathways**), and then create a careers leaflet for each one. Share your leaflets with other learners in the class so that you all have a large job search resource that you can use.

Find out about:

1. Career progression
2. How much experience is required
3. Qualifications
4. Pay scale
5. Benefits.

Functional skills

By producing a leaflet, you will be demonstrating your **English** writing skills.

Making plans

Before looking for a job, you need to gather together all the information that you have learnt in this unit, so that you will have a career plan. Read through the numbered points in the activity on page 200 and write an answer for each point. This will help you to find out about the options available and think about the type of job you should be looking for. You need to be able to answer the following questions:

- Do you know what you want to do?
- Have you found a job that you want to apply for?
- Do you have the correct qualifications for the job?
- Do you have the skills and qualities needed for the job?
- Are you going to carry on studying to get the job?
- Do you understand the terms and conditions for the job, and are you happy with them?
- Do you have an up-to-date **CV**?
- Do you have a personal skills audit?
- Do you know someone who will write you a reference?
- Will the job affect your family life?

Planning for the future

We cannot predict the future, but we need to think about it. This is done by planning for short, medium and long-term goals. For example, a short-term goal is completing a piece of work by the weekend, a medium-term goal is planning a holiday next year and a long-term goal could be wanting a family in the future. Planning for these goals requires you to know yourself and to be able to make achievable plans for the future.

✳ Key term

CV
(Curriculum Vitae)
A summary of your personal details, qualifications and experience.

◎ Activity: My goals

Write a letter to yourself that you will give to your tutor. Your tutor will give it back to you when you finish the course. In the letter, explain what your current short-term goals are, what you plan to do when the course is over, and what you would like to plan for in five years' time.

Functional skills

By writing a letter, you will be demonstrating your **English** writing skills.

✔ Check

- Planning your future is important
- You must think carefully about your qualifications
- Make sure that you have someone you can ask for a reference when you are applying for a job.

ASSESSMENT OVERVIEW

While working through this unit, you will have prepared for completing the following assessment tasks:

○	1.1	Identify jobs in different sectors of health and social care	Pages 186–191
○	1.2	Describe a job role in a health and social care setting/department	Pages 186–191
○	2.1	Describe the terms and conditions of employment for jobs in health and social care	Pages 192–193
○	3.1	Present information about qualifications and skills required for selected jobs in health and social care	Pages 194–199
○	4.1	Produce a plan to start work within health and social care	Pages 200–203

Assignment tips

- To help you pass this unit, you should produce a poster, leaflet or fact sheet that describes three job roles from different sectors of health and social care.

- Write about the work patterns, pay and benefits of the three jobs that you have chosen.

- Also write about the skills and qualities that the jobs require.

- When you have finished gathering your information, choose the most interesting job and investigate this job role further.

- Finally, carry out a personal evaluation of your own skills and qualities and decide which jobs these would make you suitable for.

HEALTH & SOCIAL CARE GROUP PROJECT

Writing a project will give you the chance to use the skills that you have learnt. You will do this piece of work as a group. You will be given a list of topics to choose from. You must choose a topic that you all find interesting. This group project will show that you can work together, that you know how to communicate, solve problems as a team and that you are self-managers.

In this unit you will:

- Find out about different aspects of health and social care jobs
- Present information as a team member using work-related skills
- Discuss your project and explain what you have found out with your tutor

What techniques can you use to find information?

205

L01 Aspects of health & social care

You will need to choose a topic for a group project that you are all interested in. Here are some suggestions.

Leisure facilities for people with disabilities

People who work in this area have to be sensitive to individual needs, they need to understand how to work with specially designed equipment, and they must provide a safe and welcoming environment where all facilities can be enjoyed by everyone, especially those with disabilities.

Menus in care homes for older people

This job involves a lot of different work skills and knowledge. The food must be tasty and nutritious and it must be interesting and give the residents choice.

Play areas for children

This is an interesting area of design work. People who build play areas for children must understand the different developmental needs that children have at different ages. The playgrounds must also be in a secure environment.

Where to find an NHS dentist

It used to be very easy to find an NHS dentist in any area, but things have changed. A lot of dentists are now private so you will have to find out about NHS Choices direct. You will also need to talk to your local primary care trust which is in charge of dentists in your area.

Drug rehabilitation schemes

You could look at the NHS Choices web page which will give you advice about where to start your investigation. It will tell you where to find your local advice centre and will explain how a key worker helps.

Access for people who use a wheelchair

Wheelchair users should have access to the same facilities as the rest of us. This means that buildings should be designed with doors that are wide enough for wheelchairs, and also access slopes.

Activity: Other places to find a project

Local TV news is a good place to start when you want to find a topic to research for your project. Watch the local news every night for a week, keep a diary of news events that are on every night and list the items that relate to health and social care. You can also investigate local facilities by looking at the programme website and your local newspaper website to see if there are any stories that may be of interest.

Most TV channels and newspapers have their own website

Check

- Always choose a subject you are really interested in for a project

- Make sure that the people you are working with are just as interested in the topic

- Use ideas or stories from the local news to start your investigation or to highlight a specific area.

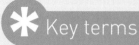 Finding information

A good project will have information that is collected in different ways. You may carry out a **questionnaire** with a number of people or hold an **interview** with one person about their experiences. Then you can use internet search engines, books and leaflets to see if everyone's experience of a service is the same.

Questionnaires

You can use a questionnaire to find out information from many people. From this you can develop a picture of what a lot of people think.

The choice of question that you use has a big effect on the type of information that you collect. There are three main types of questioning that are used in research.

1. *Yes/no questions:* this type of questioning gives the person who is answering the question a simple choice, either 'yes' or 'no'. For example if you were doing a project on nursery care, you may ask the care workers at the nursery:

'Do you think the children eat healthy food?'   Yes ☐   No ☐

If the result of the question is that three said yes and two said no, this may not be enough information because:

- You do not know what the nursery care workers think is healthy food

- You have not asked the nursery care workers if the children *only* eat healthy food

- You have not asked the parents if they serve healthy food at home.

2. *More detailed questions:* you could ask: 'Do you give children healthy snacks to eat at break time in the nursery?' Then you could ask a second question like 'Could you tell me one example of a healthy snack that you give the children?'

> What is important to you when filling out a questionnaire?

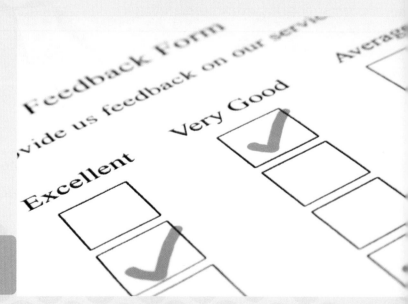

208

3. *Interviewing:* this approach can be used for one person or a small group of people. The questions are longer and need detailed answers. To do this well, send a list of questions to the person/group before you meet them. This gives them a chance to think about the answers.

Activity: Planning my time

Projects need careful planning. Imagine that you are carrying out a project with three other people. You have one month to decide on a topic, collect information, and write your project up.

1. How much time should you spend collecting information?
2. List four different ways that your group could collect information
3. How much time do you think you should all take to write up your project?

Confidentiality

Keeping information or where it came from **confidential** is an important skill that is used in health and social care. It is just as important in your project. People may be sharing information with you that they do not want to be shared with other people. You must protect them by not using their real names or making them recognisable. This will help them to trust you.

Key term

Confidentiality
Respecting information by keeping it secure and private.

Activity: Why is confidentiality important?

1. Why must we observe an individual's rights to confidentiality?
2. List three problems that could happen if you were careless with private information.

Check

- A questionnaire can use simple or more detailed questions and asks lots of people the same questions
- Planning a project is important
- Personal information should be kept confidential.

L01 Teamwork

Working as part of a team means that you can complete more work and develop more ideas than you would do on your own. When you are working together as a team, it is important that everyone agrees what you are doing and why. This will mean that you enjoy what you are doing and learn a lot about working together. This topic looks at how people work best together in teams.

What skills are important when working in a team?

Setting up a meeting

When you start your project, it is a good idea to set up a meeting. The meeting should be quite formal (this means that it is not just a chat) with an **agenda** and someone should take notes. These are called **minutes**. They are important because they are a record of what was said. Everyone has to read the minutes and agree with them before the next meeting. See page 212 for more about keeping records.

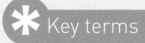

Key terms

Agenda
A list of things you want to talk about in a meeting.

Minutes
Writing down a brief summary of what was said in a meeting.

Remember

Remember to:

- Arrange a quiet room where you can have a discussion
- Use a flipchart to record your ideas
- Take minutes
- Make a list of as many areas of health and social care that you can think of, so that you all make the best possible choice for your project.

Contributing ideas and respecting others

Teams need to work well together. This means that everyone has to be able to make a contribution and to feel valued. Make sure you:

- Co-operate by sharing ideas and working together

- **Negotiate** by finding answers from talking with the group

- Respect the skills and qualities of all the team members.

Being part of a team means that you co-operate by listening to each other and seeing how everyone's ideas can fit together. If the team's ideas do not fit together, then a good team negotiates changes. A good team does this by being flexible, and by persuading other people that change is not always bad.

Key term

Negotiate
To agree on an issue after an exchange of ideas and opinions.

Case study:
Do we have the same interests?

Emma, Coral, Tammy and George are working together on their group project. Emma and Coral really want to investigate day care provision for young children. George, who loves to cook, is really interested in developing specialist meals for vulnerable individuals. Tammy doesn't really know what she wants to do yet. George has told his tutor he feels outnumbered by the others because he is a boy.

1. **What should the group do to come to a decision?**

2. **Why should Coral and Emma respect George's idea?**

3. **Should the group try to negotiate a new project topic?**

Check

- An agenda is a list of important points that need to be talked about in the meeting

- It is important to co-operate with the other team members for the best possible outcome

- Minutes are a record of the points that were made in the meeting and the points that will need further investigation.

L02 Communication skills

Communication is not just about speaking, for example you use different ways of standing and you can smile or you can look angry. You can also use written words and pictures.

You also communicate when you are listening to another person. If you do not look at them or you talk to someone else, it tells them that you are not interested in what they have to say. The way you listen to someone tells them a lot about what you think of them.

Facial expressions send out messages. What other types of communication can you think of that do not use words?

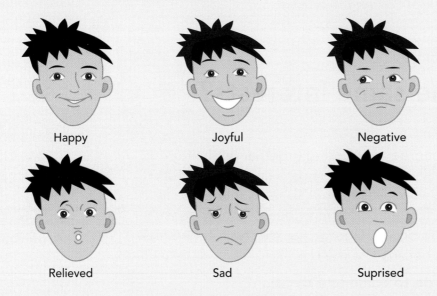

| Happy | Joyful | Negative |

| Relieved | Sad | Suprised |

Applying literacy skills

The way you place words on a page is not the same as the way you use words in everyday conversation. Words on a page are explaining important facts to the person who is reading them. You need to be clear about what you are saying. Long sentences make the person reading tired. You need to use the right information so that mistakes do not happen.

Producing clear and accurate records

Keeping a record of everything that you do is very important. Without records it is impossible to say who did what piece of work and to give them the credit for it. Taking minutes at a meeting is important because everyone has to agree that they are a correct record of what was discussed. Records of meetings must have the date, a list of who was there, who missed the meeting and what was said.

Listening and questioning skills

Learning how to listen can be difficult, because most of the time you want to do the talking. Being a good listener means you look at other people's faces and their body language. This often tells you what they are thinking, and you will know when they are going to finish what they are saying. If they do not pause, you can frown and they will see that you want to say something. A question needs to be straight to the point and clear so that people know exactly what you want to find out.

Activity: Note taking

Ask your tutor to read from a script for five minutes without stopping. At the end of the five minutes, write down as much of what they said as you can, and then check your answer against their script.

- How much did you write correctly?

- Can you summarise what your tutor said?

- Now write two questions each that you can ask to try to find the information you may have missed when your tutor was talking.

Check

- Remember that your face may be expressing something different from what you are saying

- Body language can make people feel uncomfortable or put them at their ease

- Listening carefully is an important skill that needs practise.

L02 Self-management

If you are a good team member, you are also a good self-manager. This means that you are organised and your share of the work is always done by the deadline. Here are some of the skills of a good self-manager.

Flexibility

Flexibility means being able to take different approaches to a situation.

Organising self

It is important to know what you have to do and the time you have to do it in.

Accepting responsibility

You must stand by your own decisions.

Meeting agreed deadlines and completing all set tasks on time

This is very important, because it affects the other people that you are working with.

Problem solving

You must be able to recognise when problems occur and make suggestions about how to solve them. You need to be able to think creatively to do this. This skill requires flexibility as well, because you need to be aware of all solutions.

Activity: Am I a good team member?

List the self-management skills above in order with the most important first.

Activity: Look at the mess!

Look at the mess that Coral and Emma have in front of them. Have a group discussion about what advice you would give them to sort the mess out. Use the ideas below to help you.

- *The job list*: this is probably the most important tool in your box. Remember to put a tick on the paper every time you complete a task. However, you must make sure that everyone's list is the same length and equally demanding, otherwise the people you are working with will get frustrated about what they have to do.

- *Keep a diary*: a diary is a really good way of organising yourself. It should show how much time you will spend on each part of the project. You must spend time doing this with your group members, so that you can negotiate each other's responsibilities and identify where you will need to be flexible.

- *Keep a tidy desk*: you will need to have a pile of clearly labelled books and files. Keep all of your pens and pencils in a neat container. Use a notebook for recording ideas.

Check

- Being flexible is an important self-management skill
- Being able to accept responsibility for your actions makes you a good team member
- Meeting deadlines shows that you are committed to doing a good job.

L03 Assess own work

Constructive feedback

Constructive feedback is information that is helpful and that you can learn from. It should never be one person telling another that their work is rubbish. Feedback comes from each of the group members as well as your tutor, so you need to know how you can give and receive feedback in the most positive way. Here are some tips:

- If you are giving feedback, have a clear list of the things that you want to say. This will help you to keep track of the points that you want to make, and also you can look back at your list if there are questions.

- If you are giving feedback, talk straight to the person who is receiving the feedback. Explain carefully your points, and give them time to ask questions. Try to mix positive and negative points.

- If you are receiving feedback, be positive. If you have done the best you can, then there will be some very good parts to your work.

- If you are receiving feedback, listen to what is being said. Take some paper with you to make notes in case there are questions that you may need to remember for later.

- Remember that feedback is to help you learn. We all need advice and we never stop learning.

How can examples improve feedback?

Activity: Are you fed up with feedback?

Think about how you felt when you received feedback from a tutor about previous work. Did you agree with what was said, or did you feel that the tutor was unfair?

Write a brief summary of what happened as if you were creating a scene in a play. Remember to write down how people were sitting, and whether you listened or interrupted.

Did you write down comments for later? Now write a second version showing how the experience could have been made better.

Strengths and weaknesses

Personal strengths and weaknesses are very difficult to judge for yourself and for other people. When you are applying for a job, you need to write about your strengths and weaknesses on an application form so it is a useful skill to acquire.

Activity: Did you mean what you said?

In pairs, write down your partner's strengths and weakness on a sheet of paper. Try to avoid giving examples, because this will make it personal. For example, instead of writing:

'You gave me a really good present on my birthday. Can I have another one this year?'

try: 'You are kind and generous.'

With your partner think about and discuss the way that you speak. Do you have a positive way of talking?

Check

- Feedback is important for improvement

- A diary will help you to manage your time

- Having good people skills is a strength. Making people unhappy is a weakness.

L03 Setting targets for further development

The most important outcome of any project is that you will have an idea about what you would like to do next. This may mean that you wish to improve your personal skills, such as being a better team member, or you may have been really lucky and found an area that you would like to follow up as a job.

Activity: Planning for the future

Carry out this task as if you have decided on a path for your future. This means that you must come up with a list of further areas that you need to explore, and you must think about how these will act as targets for the future.

Your final task is to prepare yourself for a mock interview. To do this, you need to think about all the different training that you have gone through as part of the course, and to write a summary of what you have learnt and where you see this knowledge taking you.

1. Why did you choose the topic that you wrote about?

2. How did you make the choice of topic?

3. Would you do it differently next time?

4. How did you choose your team?

5. How well did your team work together?

6. Were there any problems? (The interviewer will not believe you if you say that there were none.)

7. What have you learnt about working in a team?

8. What would you do differently?

Activity: Role-play

For this activity, choose a partner who worked on a different project from you, and conduct a role-play of the interview process. It is important for you to work with a person who does not have any connection to what you have done. This means that you can have some interesting discussions that will broaden your understanding of the world of health and social care. If you have a video camera, it would be useful to record your work and share it with the rest of your group. This may seem a bit scary, but if everyone does it, you will learn a lot.

Practising interview techniques

Check

- You should take time to make your decision about the topic choice for your project

- You should listen carefully to constructive criticism so that you improve your skills

- You need to be honest about any problems that may have occurred

- You must respect the thoughts of your group and pay attention to what everyone says

- You should stick to deadlines and enjoy your work.

ASSESSMENT OVERVIEW

While working through this unit, you will have prepared for completing the following assessment tasks:

○	1.1	Identify an aspect of health and social care to research	Pages 206–209
○	1.2	Work as a team member in finding relevant information	Pages 208–211
○	2.1	Use communication skills to present information clearly and accurately	Pages 212–213
○	2.2	Make a positive contribution as a team member	Pages 214–215
○	2.3	Use self-management skills to meet agreed deadlines and solve problems	Pages 214–215
○	3.1	Discuss own work-related skills in finding out about an aspect of health and social care	Pages 216–219

Assignment tips

- To help you pass this unit, you must work successfully as part of a team.

- Show that you have worked together to choose and research your topic.

- Keep evidence of your discussions, websites you have used and people you have talked to.

- Show that you have used a questionnaire.

- Show that you have dealt with problems positively, and that you have looked at a number of 'what if' scenarios to help you with your planning.

- Show that you have written an action plan that includes deadlines that you have followed.

- Produce and present a presentation about your project.

- Show evidence that you have evaluated your project and that you have responded to feedback from your tutor.

Glossary

Active listening – Showing the person you are having a conversation with that you are interested in what they have to say.

Adapted – Adjusting something to meet the needs of the users of the service and the activity.

Adolescence – The stage in a young person's life when they become sexually mature.

Agenda – A list of things you want to talk about in a meeting.

Allergies – Unusually sensitive reaction to something commonplace.

Animating – To bring something to life.

Application of IT – Using computers and information technology in a health and social care environment.

Application of number – Using numbers in a health and social care environment.

Arthritis – A medical condition that causes pain in joints, muscles and bones.

Assertive – Being confident and firm when making a point.

Assessing – Judging how well you have done.

Atmosphere – The mood and feeling of something.

Bacteria – Micro-organisms that can cause disease.

Benefits – Rewards given to employees in addition to their salary.

Biopsy – Taking a tissue sample from an individual for examination.

Braille – A form of writing for people with visual impairments that consists of raised dots and patterns that a person can read by touch.

Breach of confidentiality – Leaving information available for unauthorised people to see, or informing individuals of information when they do not need to know it.

Bullying – Treating someone badly.

Carbohydrate – Foods such as pasta, rice, bread and potatoes that provide a lot of energy.

Characteristics – Features or qualities that make a person recognisable.

Children's services – A sector of health and social care provision that focuses on the care of children.

Chiropody – Care and treatment of the feet.

Chronic respiratory disease – A long-lasting disease of the lungs.

Colleague – A person that you work with.

Commode – A movable toilet.

Community worker – Someone who works with all service users in the local area.

Confidential – Keeping information secret.

Confidentiality – Respecting information by keeping it secure and private.

Conscientiousness – Doing things properly and correctly.

Constructive feedback – Carefully considered and useful comments to help your development.

Contamination – Make unclean with poisonous or polluting substance.

Co-operation – Working together to achieve a target or goal.

Creative – Using the imagination to make new things.

Crops – Plants that are grown for the use of food.

Cross infection – Transferring infection from one place to another.

Cultural – Relating to the way that we live.

Culture – The rules we follow, the manners we have and the way we live.

CV – Curriculum Vitae

A summary of your personal details and qualifications.

Day care centre – A setting usually for older people or people with learning difficulties and disabilities to help maintain independence and provide companionship.

Dehydrated – Not having enough water in the body.

Dementia – When the brain starts to deteriorate and functions such as memory start to weaken.

Deteriorate – To slowly get worse.

Dignity – Feeling of pride or value.

Discriminate – Treating someone unfairly because of their beliefs, gender, sexuality, age orethnicity.

Empathy – Being able to identify with the situations of others and how they feel.

Emphysema – A disease in the lungs making it hard to breathe.

Employee – Someone who works for a company or organisation.

Employer – A person who pays workers to do jobs for them. Can also be known as the manager or the owner.

Enhance – To improve or increase something.

Environment – The setting you are in.

Epipen – An instrument for giving medication for allergic reactions.

Ethnicity – Belonging to a group that shares many characteristics. These characteristics can be different from other ethnicities.

Factors – Things that can influence or affect us.

Fibre – Parts of fruit, grains and vegetables that the body cannot digest, for instance bran. Fibre helps the bowels to work properly.

Fine motor skills – Small movements of the hands and fingers.

Flexible – Being able to change and adapt to different tasks and situations.

Food group – A group of foods with similar nutritional content.

Frailty – When someone is weak and their bones break easily.

Frostbite – Where body tissues, especially on the fingers, toes and nose are permanently damaged by severe cold.

Gesture – An action or movement made with the body to communicate messages.

Hazard – Anything that could potentially cause harm to someone.

Health and safety policy – The health and safety rules and regulations laid down by the employer.

Holiday time – Paid time off work.

Housebound – When someone cannot leave their house.

Human rights – Basic rights and freedoms, which all humans are allowed.

Hygiene – Maintaining high levels of cleanliness at all times to prevent the spread of disease.

Hygienic – Free from dirt and germs.

Imagination – Thinking of ideas and images in the mind.

Impairment – The loss of normal function of part of the body due to disease or injury, such as loss of eyesight.

Independence – Making your own decisions and not needing other people's help.

Indigestion – Pain or discomfort after eating food.

Infection – Disease caused by germs.

Initiative – Being able to act and make decisions without asking for help and advice.

Insurance – Money that is paid to protect in the event of something bad happening.

Interview – A conversation between two people based on a series of questions and answers.

Isolated – Feeling alone and with no family, friends or support.

Jargon – Language and words only used by particular groups.

Learning disability – A condition that prevents someone from learning basic skills or information at the same rate or to the same level as most people of the same age.

Leisure – Free time to enjoy a hobby or relaxing activity.

Literacy – The ability to read and write.

Logically – Being able to think sensibly and clearly.

Lyrics – Words of a song.

Manager – The person in charge of a setting or organisation.

Manipulation – To hold something in your hands and move it.

Medium/media – Materials used in art, such as oil paints, watercolours, pencil or collage.

Mental illness – A health condition that changes a person's thinking, feelings, or behaviour.

Micro-organism – Very small microscopic living thing. Some microorganisms cause disease.

Minutes – Writing down a brief summary of what was said in a meeting.

Mobility – Being able to move about.

Multicultural – Different groups of people from different countries, ethnic groups or religions living in the same society.

Negotiate – To agree on an issue after an exchange of ideas and opinions.

Non-toxic – Something that is not poisonous and will not cause serious harm.

Nutrients – Substances that give us nourishment.

Nutrition – The way that we take in and digest nutrients from food.

Nutritional value – The amount of nutrients provided by food.

Nutritionally balanced – Food that gives the correct balance of nutrients that the body needs.

Organisation – A company or place of work.

Parkinson's Disease – A disorder of the nervous system that makes people weak affects mobility.

Pathway – The possible direction that your career could take in the future.

Patronising – Treating someone as if they were not as clever as you.

Pay increments – How much your pay will improve over time.

Personal information – Details about you, such as your name, address, telephone number and email address.

Personal skills audit – Looking realistically at the skills that you have and whether these are the ones that you will need to do a job well.

Pharmacy

Another name for chemist shop.

Physical abuse – When someone is hit or attacked.

Physiotherapist – Professional who helps individuals gain use of particular body movements.

Policy – A guideline that tells you what to do in given situations.

Potential – Something that may be possible, but has not happened yet.

Poverty – When someone has very little money and cannot afford to buy the essentials to live a healthy life.

Practical (qualification) – Certificate that gives you day-to-day support and help with needs.

Prescription – A written note from a doctor telling a chemist what medicine to give out.

Preservatives – Chemicals that keep food eatable and drinkable for longer.

Problem solving – The process of finding an answer or solution to a problem.

Puberty – The stage when a boy or girl becomes sexually reproductive.

Public services – Services provided by the government for its people, e.g. fire service, police.

Puree – To blend or mash solid cooked food into a soft liquid.

Qualification – Gained when you successfully complete a course by passing an exam. For example, a BTEC is a vocational qualification, a GCSE is a general qualification.

Quality – A personal way of behaving that you do well.

Questionnaire – Questions used to gain information from a set of people.

Rapport – An unspoken understanding between people.

Reaction – A response to something.

Reflex – Something that happens automatically without thinking.

Repetitive strain injury (RSI) – A condition where pain and other symptoms occur as a result of repetitive use of part of the body.

Residential worker – Someone who works in care homes (for older adults or young people).

Respect – Valuing an individual or a decision they have made.

Respite – When an unpaid carer takes a break while their caring duties are covered by a paid worker.

Responsibility – When someone is trusted to carry out a job or task.

Retirement – Giving up work.

Reveal – To show something that was unclear.

Rights – Something we are allowed to have by law.

Risk – The chances of a hazard causing harm.

Risk assessment – Looking at whether an activity could cause harm and deciding whether it is safe to continue.

Rural – In the countryside.

Salary scale – The pay range for a particular type of work.

Satisfaction – Feeling pleased and happy with achievements.

Scavenger hunt – A game where you have to find a number of items on a list.

Schizophrenia – A mental illness that can affect your behaviour, thinking and emotions.

Self-management skills – This involves taking responsibility for what you do, being assertive and self-starting.

Self-starting – The ability to show that you can get on with tasks without prompting.

Shift work – Working different times on a regular basis. For example 9am to 5pm, 5pm to 1am, 1am to 9am.

Skill – Something that requires training or experience to do well in.

Social interaction – Having contact with other people.

Social skills – Being able to interact effectively with others.

Solution – An answer to a problem.

Stereotyping – When society makes assumptions about an individual or group of people.

Stimulation – Encouraging something to develop.

Subsidised – When part of the cost of something is paid by your employer.

Target – A goal to work towards.

Technique – The way in which a task is carried out.

Terminal illness – An illness that will lead to the death of the patient.

Terms and conditions – The hours that you have to work, your pay and how many days' holiday you get.

Texture – The feel and appearance of an object or surface.

Unemployed – When an individual does not have a paid job.

Unpasteurised milk – Milk that has not been treated to get rid of bacteria.

Urban – In towns or cities.

User of service – Anyone who uses health and social care services, such as a hospital patient, a child going to school or an elderly resident in a nursing home

Verbal abuse – When someone is shouted at or spoken to rudely or insultingly.

Vigilant – Keeping a look out for potential problems and dangers.

Virus – A tiny infectious particle that can cause disease.

Vitamins – Essential nutrients for the body.

Vocabulary – Set of words.

Vocational (qualification) – Qualification that teaches you skills that will help you to do a job.

Vulnerable – When an individual is at risk of harm.

Wholemeal – Foods made from brown flour, that is flour that contains bran, the hard skin of the wheat grain.

Work pattern – The hours that you have to work and when you have to carry them out.

Working conditions – The basic rights you have at work.